Receive the the Holy Spirit

Expanded Edition

"Receive the Holy Spirit."
John 20:22

Arlo F. Newell

D0851897

10951

Warner Press
ANDERSON, INDIANA

ISBN 978-1-59317-124-7

Printed in the United States of America

12 13 14 15 16 17 / EP / 10 9 8 7 6 5 4 3

Dedicated

To the Church of God congregations where the Newell family had the opportunity of experiencing the communion of the Holy Spirit and the privilege of sharing in the more excellent way of love:

Akron, Indiana
High Point, North Carolina
St. Louis, Missouri
Springfield, Ohio

Acknowledgments

I am indebted to many people as the expanded version of this book is released. Lifelong inspiration has been provided by my older brother, Marion, who modeled for me the meaning of being entirely sanctified. I was there at the altar when he claimed the experience, and his commitment has never wavered.

Second, technical guidance has been given by Joseph D. Allison and Stephen Lewis. Joe edited the original manuscript for the first edition of the book and has now made possible this new version. Stephen's editorial skills clarified the text and corrected the grammar, making the text clear and understandable.

Last but not least, I want to thank Helen, my wife of fifty-eight years, for her constant faith in me and her encouragement for me to accept the challenge of putting my convictions in writing. Without her computer skills and patience, the book would not have come to pass. Thank you, Helen, for walking with me on the Highway of Holiness; we have made the journey together.

Arlo F. Newell
May 2005

Contents

Preface to the Second Edition

Since the writing of this small volume in 1978, it has found a significant teaching ministry in the life of the church. Requests to translate the text have been received from missionaries around the world. Because of this, Warner Press has requested that it be revised and expanded for release at this time. Hearts are still hungry and souls are still seeking the deeper experience of the Spirit-filled life. It is still true: Life in the Spirit is the native climate for the Christian; it is the norm for the church.

In August of 1951, it was my privilege as a young preacher to be invited to deliver the afternoon message in the Yellow Creek Lake Camp Meeting near Beaver Dam, Indiana. Overwhelmed by the opportunity and inspired by deep conviction, I preached on the subject, "The Greatest Need of the Church." It is a message that still burns in my heart. The years have yellowed the notes of the sermon, but they have not lessened the depth of my conviction regarding this need. Periodically, I read those notes and want to say once again that the greatest need of the church is the infilling of the Holy Spirit. I believe that holiness is more than a doctrinal position or theological teaching. It is a personal experience, an experience that cleanses the heart of the believer and empowers for service, enabling us to fulfill God's purpose for our lives. The glorious church spoken of in Ephesians 5:27 can be realized only through holiness of heart and life. It is encouraging to note that in ministers' meetings, conferences, and on college campuses, one finds a renewed interest in the biblical teaching regarding God's gift of the Holy Spirit.

As we have entered the twenty-first century, the culture in which the church is called to minister challenges the biblical truth that we believe. Confronted by pluralism, secularism, and postmodernism, we are tempted to deal in theological ambiguities wherein biblical imperatives are treated as one option among multiple valid choices. In such an atmosphere, the Holy Spirit has become a shadowy figure in the twilight zone of our faith, rather than the illuminating Presence given to help us understand and appropriate the truth of God's Word.

One has only to read the book of Acts to be made acutely aware of the contrast between the church then and now. Our need is not to return to the first-century church or seek to reproduce it; to do so leads to frustration and failure. Our need is to allow the Holy Spirit to sanctify, cleanse, and empower the church, releasing us to be the church God planned for this hour.

Three concerns prompted me to agree to revise the book and write two new chapters. They are theological confusion, a twisting of the truth, and perverted power in the church. While this is not an exhaustive study, I have endeavored to bring some clarity to the theology of the Holy Spirit. In doing so, my goal has been to use terminology that is not only theologically acceptable but also generally accessible so that this text might be understandable and useful for study in small groups, prayer meetings, and church school classes.

The Church of God has endeavored to speak clearly about the Holy Spirit. Being a noncreedal people, we have done so through historical and present writings, attempting to state our position on scriptural holiness. In 1979, such a statement was issued in a small pamphlet titled *We Believe*:

"God's Church is a holy community…Through the atoning work of Christ and the sanctifying work of the Holy Spirit, the church, through the individual lives of its members, is privileged to participate in and demonstrate holiness (1 Cor 1:2; 3:17; Eph 5:25–27)."[1]

Later, in 1985, the General Assembly of the Church of God was asked to appoint a special, all-inclusive study committee "composed of qualified individuals from the academic and pastoral fields to study the work of the Holy Spirit as related to *glossolalia* in the light of Scripture, our historical perspective, and present happenings in the Church of God movement."[2] It was my privilege to serve on this committee and to participate in formulating its report, which was presented to the Assembly in 1986. I recommend the report for further study; it provides helpful understanding of the gifts of the Holy Spirit and their exercise in the life of the local congregation and personal life.

In this revised edition, two new chapters have been added to give specific attention to divine healing and church polity (governance), two areas in which misuse and abuse too often occur. Scripture refers to both of these as gifts of the Spirit. And both appear to be related to the "signs and wonders" mentioned in Acts 5:12 and Hebrews 2:4. But it is important to acknowledge that when the Holy Spirit releases God's power for signs and wonders, that release of power is always in keeping with God's Word and God's holiness. In the corporate life of the church, the gifts of the Spirit are always expressed "in a fitting and orderly way" (1 Cor 14:40), producing a harmony and symmetry that results in the beauty of holiness.

---

[1]Anderson University School of Theology, *We Believe*, 7.

[2]Callen, *Following the Light*, 300.

For those seeking signs and wonders, let me encourage you to study the Scriptures and pray for discernment before embracing such experiences or attempting to reproduce them. God's Word alone is foundational and rational, always able to stand the testing and opposition that will inevitably come.

What do I mean by the "twisting of the truth" about the Holy Spirit? Consider, as an example, two phenomena which emerge periodically when the church experiences the moving of the Holy Spirit. I refer to being "slain" in the Spirit and the "anointing" of the Spirit. At such times, it becomes difficult to distinguish between that which is scriptural and that which is emotional. Caught up in praise and worship, we can easily confuse humanly manifested phenomena with the work of the Holy Spirit. While appearing to be real, these phenomena often result in the quenching of the Spirit (1 Thess 5:19), thus preventing spiritual needs from being met. Nonscriptural practices like these not only confuse but contribute to division within the body of Christ. When such events are called into question, the divinely inspired New Testament becomes the litmus test for the experience. The Word and the Spirit continue to be the ultimate judges of these so-called manifestations of the Holy Spirit.

Scripture does not support any such action as being "slain" in the Spirit. When referring to the work and ministry of the Holy Spirit, most biblical references say, "stand up on your feet" (Ezek 2:1–2; Acts 26:16). Only misconstrued passages can be taken to imply being slain in the Spirit; sound biblical exegesis does not support it. [3]

Closely related to this erroneous teaching is the "anointing" of the Spirit. All believers in Christ have received the anointing of the Holy Spirit according to God's Word (2 Cor 1:21; 1 John 2:20, 27). In the Old Testament, such anointing was related to the enthronement of kings (e.g., Saul, David, Solomon), carrying with it recognition and the granting of divine power, authority, and protection.

However, the promise of divine power given on the day of Pentecost (Acts 1:8) has caused some to interpret the receiving of the Holy Spirit to entail a special enduement of power, enabling such anointed persons to perform miracles. Under such anointing, individuals are said to receive special revelations from God, a word of knowledge, or directions for decision making; some claim to have the power to anoint other individuals with particular gifts of healing or preaching. In such instances, the laying-on of hands by an "anointed" one is given an elevated status within the

---

[3]For further insight, please refer to Kuglin, *Handbook of the Holy Spirit*, 119.

church, which exalts the human rather than the divine. The result is that spiritual power is attributed to personalities who are in fact simply demonstrating prodigal human power, skill, and talent.

Jesus said, "The Spirit of the Lord is on me, because he has anointed me..." (Luke 4:18). Anointing is by and through the Holy Spirit. It does not come through gifted human personalities, many of whom believe they are above question because of their special giftedness. Such an attitude of spiritual autonomy is contrary to the nature of the Holy Spirit and the teachings of Christ. Our abiding relationship with Christ helps us to know that we are children of God and that therefore we "have an anointing from the Holy One" (1 John 2:20). Scripture assures us that "the anointing you received from him remains in you" (2:27). Our obedience to the Word and our abiding relationship with God is one of intelligent understanding as well as emotional attachment in worship.

As Christians, we are children of the King. As "kings and priests" (Rev 1:6; 5:10; KJV), there is an authenticity to our witness. We are entrusted with spiritual power and authority that is to be exercised responsibly. True spiritual anointing is not given so that we can rule over others, but rather to enable us to serve in humility, thus leaving no room for arrogance or self-glory because of a supposed superior anointing. Our example for true scriptural anointing is Christ, who, having all power and authority, humbled himself to serve and to save (Phil 2:5–11). Unfortunately, spiritual power received under the anointing of the Holy Spirit has too often been perverted to serve selfish goals.

Let the church be cautious of placing gifted persons on a pedestal as though they have some special anointing, lest we cause them to sin piously. God is not a respecter of persons (Acts 10:34). All believers have received the anointing that they might be able to know truth from error and to know that any teaching above and beyond that which Christ has revealed is irrelevant and dangerous.

It is my hope that this introduction to the revised edition conveys my deep desire to live a life of holiness and to encourage others to find the joy of the sanctified life. There is no greater joy than to know Christ as both Savior and Lord, to know that the past is forgiven and that each day you walk with him. This daily walk will inevitably lead to a life of holiness. God's Word speaks with an ever-increasing illumination, an ever-expanding understanding of what it means to walk in the Spirit (Gal 5:25). Do not settle for the littleness of legalism or the peril of pessimism. Dare to seek and to find, to knock, knowing that the door to fullness of faith will be opened. Go on to perfection! When writing of Christian perfection, John Wesley did not mean the perfection of performance but the purity of intent—to be all that God intended for you to be in his likeness. Let the desire of your heart be to be like Jesus—that is holiness as God intended.

What do I desire for this revised edition? Do I have a vision for this book? Yes. First, that the words contained herein will clearly reveal that the greatest need of the church is the infilling of the Holy Spirit. Second, that the writer, who is still seeking and finding new truth regarding holiness, will be able to inspire others to desire to be wholly sanctified (1 Thess 5:23).

Finally, let me give my personal testimony, using Paul's words:

> I have not yet reached the highest life, nor am I yet perfect. But I keep pressing forward to make that life my own, just as Christ made me His own. I do not claim that I have hold of that highest life yet. But one thing I do. Forgetting the things I have left behind, I reach forward to the things that are ahead. I press on and up toward the finishing line. I am trying for the prize; God through Christ Jesus is calling me to come on up (Phil 3:12–14, Laubach).

Accept the challenge: Receive the Holy Spirit!

Arlo F. Newell
Anderson, Indiana
March 2005

Preface to the First Edition

This book records one pilgrim's progress in quest of the Holy Spirit. Rather than a journal, it is a study of God's revelation of the Spirit throughout Scripture. In reality, it is an attempt to share with others what the writer has discovered about life in the Spirit.

For years, I wrestled with the theological term *sanctification*. While having heard sermons preached and testimonies given, it was difficult always to find models of the experience over sin and self. Questions began to arise and doubts obscured my spiritual understanding. Then came the glorious truth about the Holy Spirit dwelling within the lives of believers, sanctifying and equipping them to serve God victoriously. I also witnessed that kind of life being lived by persons who had been confronted by great conflict. They experienced all the struggles that everyone else faced—sometimes even more—and yet remained surrendered to God's perfect will. This type of faith was attractive to me, and as a young Christian, I claimed the sanctifying experience of the Holy Spirit in the summer of 1946. No, it was not like anyone else's experience, nor were there any great events that took place—only the reality that God had fulfilled his promise and that the Holy Spirit reigned within my heart.

However, great confusion exists today in regard to our theology of the Holy Spirit. The ominous silence about the Holy Spirit in many pulpits is frightening when one remembers the words of the late Charles Ewing Brown, former editor of the *Gospel Trumpet* (now *Vital Christianity*). In his book *The Meaning of Sanctification*, he wrote: "The doctrine of entire sanctification is an heroic doctrine. It requires a spiritual church and ministry for its acceptance, promotion, development, and successful growth. *It always tends to die out in a worldly church*, but it will kindle a flame of fire in every community where it is accepted, witnessed to, and lived out in experience."[1]

We may measure where we are spiritually by that statement. Our silence on this vital subject could be an indictment against the incipient decay of worldliness that seeks to make inroads into the church. On the other hand, the statement could challenge us to rethink our theology on the Holy Spirit and thus kindle a flame that would produce revival across the Movement.

Our message of the Holy Spirit has not changed. It is valid for this hour in God's church. We are a holiness people in the highest and most noble meaning of that term. Therefore, let us leave to future generations not merely institutions; let us leave a lasting legacy of the Spirit of truth.

Arlo F. Newell
Anderson, Indiana
June 1978

---

[1]Brown, *Meaning of Sanctification*, xvi, italics added.

The earth was formless and void,
and darkness was over the surface of the deep,
and the *Spirit of God* was moving over the surface of the waters.
Then God said, "Let there be light";
and there was light.

—GENESIS 1:2–3, NASB

MEET
GOD'S
REPRESENTATIVE

God's major goal in creation past and present is to create His own people and an appropriate environment for them. The essential goal of the people of God is to bear their Creator's image in holiness, righteousness, love and wisdom.

Eugene E. Carpenter
"The Handiwork of God in Natural Creation," 149

1

Meet God's Representative

GOD'S HOLY SPIRIT is moving among us today! We see him evidenced in those things that have always been characteristic of God's activity in human history. In the Old Testament, his work is the creative movement of Genesis, the life-giving breath of Ezekiel, the power of deliverance in Exodus, the judgment wine of Hosea—but it is always a power controlled of God. Within the New Testament, his work is seen as the promise of the Father in Luke, the baptismal dove of Matthew, the Comforter of John, the wind of God in Acts, the fruit of the Spirit in Galatians, the gifts of the Spirit in Corinthians, and the invitation of Revelation as God invites all to come. Just as surely as he was actively involved in human history in the past, he is active in the renewal of God's people today. Parachurch groups empowered by the Holy Spirit reach the world with good news. Mission strategy stirs the soul, sending out laborers into the vineyard. Revival among the people of God welds us together in Christian unity and ministry to human need. God has truly turned loose upon the world the power revealed in the person of the Holy Spirit.

But as is so often the case, many have not really met him personally. We know about his works, for we have seen how the Spirit's power can revive the church. His gifts (*charismata*, 1 Cor 12) are being demonstrated daily among God's people. The fruit of the Spirit (Gal 5:22) is enjoyed as we experience it relationally as believers in Christ. And yet, it is comparable to knowing about an individual's power of leadership, knowing of his talents and abilities, even knowing something of his relationship with others, but never meeting the person. So it is with the Holy Spirit. Too much of our information has come to us secondhand. Speaking to his generation, Samuel Chadwick wrote: "The church still has a theology of the Holy Ghost, but it has no living consciousness of his presence and power."[1] More recently, William Barclay has written: "For the most part it remains true that our thinking about the Spirit is vaguer and more undefined than our thinking about any other part of our Christian faith."[2] Because of this, let us seek to discover who the Holy Spirit really is.

To introduce us to the Holy Spirit, God has given a progressive revelation of this truth. He always begins where we are and leads us to a more complete understanding of his nature. Beginning with the Hebrew people, God presented the Spirit in a manner which they would understand. The Hebrew mind sought first to know God. To Israel, life was wrapped up in the action of God, a God who had acted in their history, invading the world with his presence. Thus the doctrine or teaching of the Holy Spirit grew out of the life situation of the people of God. The Old Testament becomes, thus, a prologue to the more complete revelation of the Holy Spirit as set forth in the New Testament.

As the Breath of God

While the term *Holy Spirit* appears only three times in the Old Testament, the related terms translated as "spirit" and "Spirit of God" appear in abundance. Early usage carries the connotation of the "breath of life," that supernatural power and energy which is given only by God. Israel was vitally concerned about the action of God performed by the Spirit. Therefore, when God's action was recognized in deliverance or in prophetic utterance, it was natural to speak of the Spirit's bringing it to pass.

The life-giving power of the Spirit is manifested in passages such as Genesis 1:2, where we are told the "Spirit of God was moving over the face of the waters" (NASB). In the acts of creating and giving life, the "breath" or "wind" of God was active.[3] Of great significance is the understanding that the Spirit entered into and controlled the prophets as forth-tellers of God. Micah is only one of the many who expressed this type of Spirit-possessed life. "But truly I am full of power by the spirit of the LORD," he wrote (3:8, KJV).

Spirit-filled people were different! They were controlled by a power beyond themselves, accomplishing more than they could have achieved

---

[1]Chadwick, *Way to Pentecost*, 12.

[2]Barclay, *Promise of the Spirit*, Foreword.

[3]See also Job 33:4; Ps 104:30; Ezek 37:5–6.

in human ability alone. The Spirit provided them with strength, wisdom, patience, and inspiration. The Spirit gave life, provided power, and gave victory to God's servants.

In the Ministry of Christ

Too often in studies of the Holy Spirit, we have placed his ministry in a post-Pentecost chronology. However, with this brief insight into the Old Testament concepts, one can easily see why the writers of the Gospels could have spoken of the Spirit's action in the total plan of redemption. They saw the Holy Spirit as a person ministering for God in the world. Rather than an impersonal force, he is a person with all the qualities of life. It is even possible to discourage him through disobedience and rejection (1 Thess 5:19). His nature is divine and he seeks to exalt the Christ (John 15:26), thus glorifying the Father (John 17:1). To speak of the Holy Spirit as an "it" or to refer to a particular "power" is to err in rightly understanding the Spirit representing God in the world. God has revealed himself in a person, the Holy Spirit, expressed in the personality of his Son, Jesus Christ.

All of the Synoptic Gospel writers bear witness to the involvement of God's representative in the ministry of Jesus. The whole presentation is linked with Old Testament prophecies such as Isaiah 42:1: "Here is my servant...I will put my Spirit on him." Following Jesus' baptism, the Holy Spirit testified to God's approval (Matt 3:16–17) and led the Christ into the wilderness temptations, giving him strength to triumph over evil through the Word. Again, Christ's active ministry is prefaced by his declaration "The Spirit of the Lord is on me..." (Luke 4:18). Through the Spirit, Christ received direction and was equipped for his servant role in the world. The basic ideas are carried over from the Hebrew tradition— life, power, and God's witness through a person possessed by the Spirit.

As the Counselor

Before leaving the Gospels, one must note that the writer of the gospel of John moves beyond Matthew, Mark, and Luke in his account of the Spirit's action. Here too the Spirit is related to the new birth (3:5–6), thus bringing life. But John presents also the promise of the fullness of the Spirit, which would abundantly satisfy all humanity (7:37–39). To John, the Spirit is the *paraclete* (14:16; 15:26; 16:7), one who stands by your side to enable you to face life and eternity. A Comforter, yes. A Counselor, yes. But much more than these words can convey to our human minds.

The Holy Spirit not only comforts but bears the burden with you. He not only counsels but walks beside you to give direction, provides strength to carry the burden, and then pleads your case before the Father. In John 14, the Spirit is referred to as the gift given to those who love Christ and keep his commandments (vv. 15–16). This part of our study is vital to a right understanding of God's representative. We do not earn the Spirit; he is given to those who supremely love God and keep his commandments.

The Counselor is the "Spirit of truth" (14:17), and he will "teach you all things, and will remind you" (14:26) of all that Jesus said. As the Spirit of truth, he will also bear witness to Christ (15:26), and he will guide us "into all truth" (16:13). The implications of this dimension of the Spirit's ministry are unlimited. Because of his presence and leadership, there need be no stagnant saints or spiritual stalemates in the church. There are depths of truth that only he can reveal to the searching hearts of Christian disciples.

Desiring to know God and to receive the promised gift of the Father, the apostles obediently waited (Acts 1:4), presenting themselves before the Lord to be used of him as witnesses. Already they were God's people, seeking to be obedient, to do his will. It was upon such persons that the Holy Spirit fell.

As the Wind of God

When God is rightly represented, all human personalities are overshadowed by his power and presence. So it was on the day of Pentecost. How does one describe such a divine demonstration of God's manifestation? Human words, even Greek ones, seem insufficient. Luke, therefore, turns to symbolic language to tell of the outpouring of the Holy Spirit (Acts 2:1–4).

One must guard against reading into this text more than is really stated, but three things are quite clear. This outpouring of the Spirit is symbolized by (1) a sound like the "blowing of a violent wind," (2) "tongues of fire," and (3) speaking "in other tongues." From the opening verses of Genesis, the "wind" of God has moved and now comes to separate the chaff from the grain. The "wind" also brings the freshness of rain and the promise of abundant harvest. Luke recognizes within this experience the fire of purification, purging those things that would hinder the progress of the young church. Pentecost both teaches and demonstrates the purifying aspect of the work of the Holy Spirit, God's representative in experiential holiness.

The part of the event at Pentecost that has caused considerable concern through the ages (note Paul's concern in 1 Cor 14) is the speaking "in other tongues." Let it suffice to say that it symbolized the gift of communication. God enabled these Spirit-filled persons to share with others this fulfillment of prophecy (Joel 2:28–32), giving validity to the life, death, and resurrection of Christ. If God was to be rightly revealed in Christ and represented through the presence of the Holy Spirit, all people must be able to understand the message. For that very reason, the universality of the gospel is demonstrated in this means.

As surely as the "wind" of God moved upon the face of the deep, demonstrating God's power in creation, he now breathes upon these believers and life is breathed into the young church, the new Israel, the people of God. The newness of this life is evident in the fact that this experience produces a new community of faith, a fellowship of the Holy Spirit, the church of God. In the power of the Spirit, they would now go forth with a holy boldness to witness to God's love and his plan of redemption.

The passion of the Pauline writings is summed up in one phrase: the Spirit-filled life. It becomes the pulsebeat of the writer; references to it occur about 120 times in his epistles. For that reason alone, we direct our attention in this chapter to only two areas of concern: the fruit of the Spirit and the gifts of the Spirit.

As the Enabler from God

As God's representative, the Holy Spirit seeks to reveal the very nature of God in attitudes and relationships. Therefore, Paul informs us that the life controlled by the flesh will produce the sins of the flesh (Gal 5:19–21). But a Spirit-filled life produces a nature akin to God. The fruit of the Spirit is not produced through human effort but through a life yielded to God. Thus a person experiences "love, joy, peace, patience, kindness, goodness, faithfulness, gentleness and self-control" (Gal 5:22–23). A more complete study of these divine characteristics will be given in succeeding chapters.

God's representative not only enables us to share in his nature but also equips us to participate in his ministry (Eph 4:7–14). Therefore, the gifts of the Spirit as listed in Romans 12, 1 Corinthians 12, and Ephesians 4 are not exhaustive; but they do become representative of God's plan to enable the members of the Body to serve him effectively. Each believer has an important role to fill, and grace is given to each of us "according to the measure of the gift of Christ" (Eph 4:7, KJV). Paul saw in the gifts that which went beyond human talent and ability. Certainly, one's God-given abilities are not to be ignored, but the gifts of the Spirit are not dependent upon these alone. Most important are the words found in 1 Corinthians 12:31: "But eagerly desire the greater gifts. And now I will show you the most excellent way." Paul herein admonishes us to seek that perfect love, which will enhance every other gift. Prophecy, tongues, and knowledge will all pass away, but the gift of perfect love will remain. This love—the very nature of God, for God is love—is "poured out…into our hearts by the Holy Spirit" (Rom 5:5).

A word of caution is helpful as we reflect upon this brief introduction to God's representative, the Holy Spirit. In an hour of history, wherein great emphasis is placed upon the experiential level of learning, we would be wise to measure the value of such experience by the authority of God's Word. In seeking for a particular experience, many have failed to find the authentic and the real. While desiring a special gift, they have failed to receive God's gift in the person of the Holy Spirit. The late Samuel Chadwick, in his Christian classic, *The Way to Pentecost*, gives his testimony of seeking to know the Holy Spirit:

> The blessing I sought was power. The blessing God had for me began farther in and deeper down. Power was conditioned. The Truth that sanctifies begins with cleansing of heart and motive, a life surrendered to the Divine Will, and a personality possessed by and filled with the Holy Spirit, and I *very nearly missed the way*.[4]

God has placed his representative in the world that you might know him. Together we have begun our quest; let us not stop short of a deep personal relationship with God, which must always eventuate in the fullness of the Holy Spirit. We dare not miss the way! Let us go on unto perfection (Heb 6:1, KJV)!

FOR FURTHER STUDY:

1. Why is there such a renewed interest in the theology of the Holy Spirit?

2. Of what significance is the study of the personality of the Holy Spirit?

3. In what manner did the Spirit come upon individuals in Old Testament times?

---

[4]Chadwick, *Way to Pentecost*, 106, italics added.

4. Look up and consider these Old Testament passages about the Spirit of God: Ezekiel 36:25–27; Malachi 3:1–3; and Joel 2:28–29.

5. What New Testament words are used to reveal the nature of the Holy Spirit?

6. Why do some people refer to the book of Acts as the Acts of the Holy Spirit?

The *wind* blows wherever it pleases.
You may hear its sound, but you cannot tell where it comes from
or where it is going.
So it is with everyone born of the *Spirit.*

—JOHN 3:8

GOD'S REVELATION OF THE REAL

Nicodemus did not know that night where the wind of the Spirit *was one day going to carry him. Perhaps some of us would think twice before praying for the gift of the Spirit if we knew where He was liable to lead us. But it is thrilling too. For you see, it means you just cannot tell what God may yet make of your life and character.*

James S. Stewart
The Wind of the Spirit, 18
(emphasis added)

2

God's Revelation of the Real

THE BIBLE is God's revelation of himself through the written word. It validates his representative in the world as a personality with all his divine attributes. How marvelous that the writers of both Testaments bear witness to the Spirit's distinctive presence, power, and purpose in God's plan of redemption. And yet how tragic that humanity has not been able to recognize the real from the unreal in regard to this great truth. This only accentuates the fact that there are some things that are beyond human comprehension. Charles Carter, in his book *The Person and Ministry of the Holy Spirit,* comments:

> man's finite mind, or human limitations, can never fully comprehend the infinity or limitlessness of divinity is obvious. To comprehend God fully would necessitate that man himself possess the limitless wisdom of God, in which unthinkable event he would no longer be man, but God.[1]

Because of this, the inspired writers have chosen symbols to help us understand the reality of the Holy Spirit. Within the Bible, one finds truth conveyed through metaphors, similes, types, parables, and allegories; each one helps us to know the reality of God through revelation. Many of these expressions help us to understand better the nature of the Holy Spirit, whom we seek to know in his fullness. In this chapter, let us consider briefly only three of these expressions: reality revealed through the wind, the fire, and the seal of the Spirit.

---

[1]Carter, *Person and Ministry,* 27.

The Wind of God

Even theologians, with their well-reasoned knowledge of God, do not always comprehend the reality of the Holy Spirit. Nicodemus was such a scholar in search of reality. He knew well the religious ritualism of his faith, but he sought the reality of personal experience. His insatiable desire to experience reality moved him to seek Jesus at night. Articulating his desire to the master teacher, he heard Jesus respond by speaking of the necessity of being "born again" (John 3:3). In amazement, Nicodemus sought to comprehend the depth of meaning in this statement. "How can a man be born when he is old?" he asked (3:4). Then Jesus, using an illustration understood by all, said, "The wind blows wherever it pleases. You hear its sound, but you cannot tell where it comes from or where it is going. So it is with everyone born of the Spirit" (3:8).

This illustration became the means of revealing the reality of the Holy Spirit. It was as though Jesus said: "The Spirit of God is just like that— invisible yet unmistakable, impalpable yet full of power, able to do wonderful things for you if only you will stand in its path and turn your face to it and open your life to its influence."[2]

All of the tradition of Nicodemus' religious background began to take on significance. The "breath" or "wind" of God (*ruach* in the Hebrew) seemed to spring to life in his heart as he began to comprehend what this rabbi was saying. The Holy Spirit is like the wind of God—that which cannot be stereotyped by spiritual sophistication, trapped by traditionalism, or boxed in by narrow beliefs. God's representative has been released in the world to minister as he wills.

The Fire of God

"They saw what seemed to be tongues of fire that separated and came to rest on each of them" (Acts 2:3). These words from the inauguration of the early church convey to us God's expectation for the purity of his people. As a witness to the outpouring of the Holy Spirit, he made it both congregational and personal. There was only one fire, but it sat upon each of them. While we are all members of the body of Christ, there is the reality of an experience in the Holy Spirit for every believer. Christ's disciples had already experienced the Spirit in regeneration; now God revealed the reality of the Holy Spirit through purification, the cleansing of their inward nature.

Fire had long been recognized as a symbol of God's power to remove all foreign elements from one's life. Malachi had spoken of the refiner's fire

---

[2]Stewart, *Wind of the Spirit*, 10.

that purified the gold (3:3), and now the reality of that experience came into fulfillment through the Spirit. While already converts to Christ, there remained within the hearts of these believers attitudes and desires that needed to be cleansed. Jealousy, competition, and selfishness kept them from being greatly used of God. As a boy, I recall the prayer-meeting crowd singing:

> Let the fire fall on me,
> Let the fire fall on me;
>   The fire of Pentecost,
>   consuming sin and dross,
> Let the holy fire from heaven fall on me.[3]

The coming of the Holy Spirit into the life of the believer cleanses the heart of those elements that would be contrary to the nature of Christ. As a consuming fire, he enters your life; his fullness permeates your very being, sanctifying you entirely (1 Thess 5:23). While not making it impossible to sin, the presence of the Holy Spirit in your life makes it possible to live victoriously over sin.

Nothing is more real than the illumination that comes through the abiding presence of the Holy Spirit. As a pillar of fire, God had given guidance to the children of Israel as he led them through the desert wilderness. And while we are pilgrims and strangers in this world, the illuminating presence of the Holy Spirit will lead us on the highway of holiness. While education may equip us to know the Word of God intellectually, it does not enable us to understand the Word experientially. Paul wrote, "The man without the Spirit does not accept the things that come from the Spirit of God, for they are foolishness to him, and he cannot understand them, because they are spiritually discerned" (1 Cor 2:14). God, through the Holy Spirit, enables all persons who earnestly seek him to know this experience. Jesus said, "When he, the Spirit of truth, comes, he will guide you into all truth" (John 16:13). This is an age of spiritual illiteracy. While having abundant opportunities to know the truth, we live in spiritual darkness, desperately in need of the illuminating presence of the Holy Spirit.

For every believer, obedience to Christ requires that we "walk in the light, as he is in the light" (1 John 1:7). To do this would mean that he, the Holy Spirit, would give us understanding about these things: the authority of his Word, deliverance from sin, stewardship of possessions, true

---

[3]William J. Henry, "Let the Fire Fall on Me," in *Worship the Lord,* 483.

Christian unity, divine physical healing, the end of time, and the resurrection from the dead. We are not dependent upon human interpretation but upon divine revelation through the Holy Spirit as he illuminates our understanding of the Word of God.

Years ago, it was my privilege to hear Ralph Cushman, bishop in the United Methodist Church. God's Word still speaks to the human heart through Cushman's writings because he walked in the illuminating presence of the Holy Spirit. In revivals and camp meetings, I have shared these lines from his little book, *I Have a Stewardship*. The words are my prayer for the church:

> *Set us afire, Lord,*
>   *Stir us, we pray!*
> *While the world perishes*
>   *We go our way,*
> *Purposeless, passionless,*
>   *Day after day,*
> *Set us afire, Lord,*
>   *Stir us, we pray!*[4]

God is able to purify your heart and illuminate your mind as you discover the reality of the Holy Spirit in your life.

The Seal of the Spirit

With an enlarged understanding through the wind and fire, we seek some validation regarding the Holy Spirit. What evidence do we have regarding the reality of this experience? God's promise to his children and his plan for all to be redeemed will be helpful in satisfying this quest.

In Ephesians, Paul writes of new life in Christ. Reference is made to God's plan that all people "should be holy and without blame before him in love" (1:4, KJV). This, he notes, is through an experience made possible through the blood of Christ and validated by the "seal" of the Holy Spirit. Verses 13–14 read:

> And you also were included in Christ when you heard the word of truth, the gospel of your salvation. Having believed, you were marked in him with a seal, the promised Holy Spirit, who is a deposit guaranteeing our inheritance until the redemption of those who are God's possession—to the praise of his glory.

---

[4]Cushman, *I Have a Stewardship*, 30.

Being children of God (Rom 8:16–18), we have entered into the blessings of the Christian life in this world while living in anticipation of the life to come. For Paul, this *seal* of the Holy Spirit helped him to have an eternal perspective, to see beyond this life, enabling him to claim the promises God has given to all of his children. Notice Paul's use of the word *all* as relating to the reality of the seal of the Spirit. In Romans 8:9, Paul places priority on surrender to the Spirit. "And if anyone does not have the Spirit of Christ, he does not belong to Christ." But this very experience of being "in Christ" helps us to look at "all things" from a totally different view. That assurance gave confidence to Paul, this intrepid missionary, making him a kind of practical optimist. Even in times of adversity, the seal of the Spirit enabled him to say, "And we know that in *all things* God works for the good of those who love him, who have been called according to his purpose" (Rom 8:28).

In our humanity, we rebel against that by questioning the tragedies and heartaches of life—the tragic death of a loved one, the handicap of an innocent child, or the suffering of a faithful saint of God in old age. How does one face these unanswerable questions of the hour? Paul was able to see beyond them because the seal of the Holy Spirit enabled him to claim the promises of God regarding the future. He actually believed that, while here, we see through a glass dimly—there, in God's tomorrow, we will see face-to-face. The Holy Spirit gave him that assurance. Paul uses these words once again in the closing verses of this eighth chapter of Romans: "In *all these things* we are more than conquerors through him who loved us" (8:37). In his humanness, Paul was subject to all of these things— tribulation, distress, persecution, famine, nakedness, peril, and sword. But he had God's promise that love would overcome. His source of victory is no secret, for the seal of the Holy Spirit still bears witness to the truth of the Word that God's people through faith shall ultimately triumph over death, sin, and the world.

The third reference to the Pauline words *all things* is found in 1 Corinthians 3:21–23. "All things are yours, whether Paul or Apollos or Cephas or the world or life or death or the present or the future—all are yours, and you are of Christ, and Christ is of God."

Within the heart of this saint, God had given the witness—the "seal" of the Holy Spirit. He really believed that God had given to us "all things." It is true that some are yet to be experienced and received, but they will come to pass. The meek will inherit the earth! The pure in heart shall see God! This mortal shall put on immortality—in a moment, in the twinkling of an eye—and we shall be caught up to be with the Lord (1 Cor 15:52–54; 1 Thess 4:17). Not in some seven-year period of rapture, but rather "we will be with the Lord *forever*" (1 Thess 4:17). The Holy Spirit bears witness as the seal and earnest of God's Word.

Yes, more real than the tangible things of life are the things of faith. Paul states that that which is real is not that which is seen but that which is not seen. Those things that we clutch so tightly can be lost so easily. But the things of the Spirit—faith, hope, and love—are lasting. While being revealed throughout the Bible through symbols, nothing is more real than the experience of the Holy Spirit. Bernard Ramm, speaking of this quest for reality, wrote:

> The biblical answer is that the hardest reality is spirit, that the realest of realities is spirit, that the most enduring of realities is spirit, and that the most powerful of realities is spirit. Here then is the modern paradox. That which modern man thinks is the most ethereal and insubstantial of all that he can think of—spirit—is from the Christian standpoint the greatest of all realities. For were it not for the Word of God and the Spirit of God this great universe in its microscopic and macroscopic dimensions would not only have no reality at all, but it would not exist at all. If we want to get down to bedrock of hard reality, we have to get down to the Spirit of God.[5]

Allow the breath of God to breathe upon you, the fire of God to cleanse you, and the seal of the Spirit to assure you of this reality.

FOR FURTHER STUDY:

1. This chapter has listed only three symbols or emblems of the Holy Spirit. Find scriptural basis for other symbols applicable to this revelation.

2. In what way does God lead us by the light of the Holy Spirit?

3. If the wind of God brings freshness and newness to our lives, is it possible for Spirit-filled persons to become spiritually stale or unproductive? Consider the reasons why.

---

[5]Ramm, *Rapping about the Spirit*, 20.

4. In what aspects of our spiritual lives do the words *cleanse* or *purify* apply to this experience in the Holy Spirit?

5. Is there a difference in Scripture between the meaning of the "seal" of the Spirit and the "deposit" ("earnest" in the KJV) of the Spirit?

6. What passages of Scripture would you use to refute arguments that the seal of the Spirit implies eternal security?

And the very God of peace sanctify you *wholly*;
and I pray God your *whole* spirit and soul and body
be preserved blameless
unto the coming of our Lord Jesus Christ.

—1 Thessalonians 5:23, KJV

THE
WHOLENESS
OF
HOLINESS

The real test of Holiness is deliverance from sin *and not deliverance from personal dispositions, and peculiar manifestations, which may be as numerous and as diverse as the persons involved. These manifestations have to do with our* "peculiar temperament" *and not with our hearts' moral condition.*

Roy S. Nicholson
Holiness and the Human Element, 146
(emphasis added)

33

3

The Wholeness of Holiness

THE REALITY of our faith reveals to us the holiness of God. More than a descriptive adjective, telling what he is like, *holiness* reveals the very nature of his being. It speaks of his transcendency over all creation, of his awesome glory and his impeccable character. Angelic beings praised him, saying, "Holy, holy, holy is the LORD Almighty; the whole earth is full of his glory" (Isa 6:3). And through the inspired writers God revealed his desire that we, too, share in his holiness. The Old Testament writer of Leviticus declared: "I am the LORD your God: consecrate yourselves and be holy, because I am holy" (11:44).

This same truth was proclaimed to the early church in the epistle of 1 Peter: "But just as he who called you is holy, so be holy in all you do; for it is written: 'Be holy, because I am holy'" (1:15–16).

Rather than being an impossible dream for the child of God, the experience of holiness needs to be viewed as God's plan for his people and made possible through the person of the Holy Spirit.

His Holiness Reveals Our Brokenness

Basic to our understanding of holiness is the concept of wholeness and completeness. God does not do things by halves. He does not leave his revelation or his redemption unfinished. And nothing is more contradictory to Christian theology than disunity, disharmony, and discord among those professing to know Christ. While knowing this theologically, we have experienced great difficulty in expressing it practically. The community of faith is plagued with broken relationships, fragmented families, and spiritual schisms.

Everett L. Cattell, in his book *The Spirit of Holiness*, has written: "One of the most serious criticisms made against 'holiness sects' is their predisposition to strife and division."[1] Whether in holiness sects or in major religious denominations, it is a contradiction to biblical theology to see the people of God divided. Division is a sin! It is like a demonic disease, crippling the effectiveness of the church's witness. *Disease* has been simply defined as "dis-ease." When there is no unity, no peace, and no wholeness of integrated Christian faith, there is need for holiness. The blood of Christ brings peace for the guilt-ridden soul. The mind of Christ brings peace to the troubled intellect. The virtue of Christ brings healing to the afflicted body. Holiness is the way to wholeness in every area of your being as a person.

If you are struggling with inner turmoil, the inability to accept yourself and to relate properly to others, this chapter is for you. God is not merely a spiritual guru, ministering through meditation and mental gymnastics. He is the God of reality, ministering to your total personality. Forgiveness of sins is foundational, but God has also planned for the total redemption of your life. Referred to as a holistic approach to theology, it simply means that God is concerned about every aspect of your life. He desires, not merely to prepare you for heaven, but to help you live victoriously over sin in this present life.

A God of Completeness

The perfect plan of salvation from sin was formulated, Peter states, "before the creation of the world" (1 Peter 1:20). Perfection implies wholeness. Nothing is missing! When God viewed his creation, he measured it for its unity, harmony, symmetry, and beauty, and said, "It is good" (see Gen 1:31). Salvation history reveals that God fulfilled all of his promises in this same manner. He kept his covenant with Abraham. He did raise up a people for his name. And he did send the promised Messiah. Paul wrote, "When the time had fully come, God sent his Son, born of a woman, born under law, to redeem those under law" (Gal 4:4–5). All of this was foretold by the prophets and made possible the complete redemption of humanity. The account of Christ on Calvary speaks of the holiness of God. His cry of fulfillment, "It is finished!" (John 19:30) denotes the fact that the whole plan of redemption had been completed. The Greek word used in this account is *teleos,* meaning a completed act. Christ did not stop short of the fulfillment of God's perfect will. Holiness centers in com-

---

[1] Cattell, *Spirit of Holiness,* 70.

pleteness. Christ was and is the perfect sacrifice; none other need ever be made. Every believer in Christ has entered into the "everlasting covenant," and the extent of the work of redemption is limitless.

The writer of Hebrews states: "He is able to save completely those who come to God through him" (7:25).

Understanding of the word *completely* applies not to how long he saves, but to the depth or degree to which he is able to save. The extent of saving grace goes beyond the initial forgiveness of sin to the sanctifying of our very nature by the infilling of the Holy Spirit. Many persons, having been born again, find themselves struggling with divided desires, undisciplined appetites, and strained interpersonal relationships. While having found forgiveness of sin, they have not been able to find the peace of God that is available through the Holy Spirit. Questions arise, like, Must I continue this war within? Is there no peace in Christ other than this knowledge of forgiveness? Does he only save me *in* my sin? or Can I be set free *from* my sin? While not a panacea for spiritual ills, holiness does provide an answer to these questions, for all of them deal with the wholeness that can be ours.

Sanctification of the Whole Person

Paul, having experienced this struggle in his own soul, wrote to the Christians in Thessalonica. Without question, he affirmed that this unifying experience of holiness is God's will for every believer (1 Thess 4:3). God has called us not only to conversion but to the wholeness of holiness (4:7). Being so concerned for these Christians whom he loves, Paul prays: "And the very God of peace sanctify you wholly; and I pray God your *whole* spirit and soul and body be preserved blameless unto the coming of our Lord Jesus Christ" (5:23, KJV). The use of the word *wholly* is indicative of the completeness of his work of grace. Having experienced new life in Christ through being born again by the Holy Spirit, the believer finds within a hunger for holiness. Redemption has restored in the creature the image of the Creator. Now the desire is to do his will and become more and more like him in true holiness. This quest for more of God's likeness brings each person to a deeper experience of divine grace.

Dr. Paul S. Rees, beloved world Christian, has said that "too often we have become connoisseurs of terms, rather than consumers of truth." He is correct in that too often we place the emphasis on terminology rather than theology. Truth is truth, whether we call it sanctification, second-blessing holiness, or, in the words of John Wesley, "perfect love." Of this we may be sure, there is a crisis experience in the Holy Spirit beyond initial conversion which makes possible the wholeness of the child of God. This experience deals with the "whole man including his intellect, emotion, will, and his body as far as it is under the control of his will in voluntary actions. The holy man is the whole man, integrated, harmonized within by his supreme, inclusive purpose to realize in himself and others the moral image of God revealed in Christ, God incarnate."[2]

Please Be Patient—God Is Not Finished with Me Yet

The first-century church experienced this complete filling of the Holy Spirit. While being made possible by the blood of Christ (Heb 13:12), this sanctification (setting apart) was the result of divine human interaction, involving the human will to consent and God's power to sanctify. Dr. Ralph Earle says, "The common usage of the two terms leads us to affirm that a *human* consecration is the prerequisite for a *divine* sanctification."[3] Consecration is more than an emotional response to religious ecstasy. It is the instantaneous, willful, decisive act of surrender on the part of God's child—forevermore yielding every avenue of one's being to the control of the Holy Spirit. Such a commitment does not end with one glorious moment, but is a continuing, growing experience of obedience to God's will. While claimed instantaneously by faith, it is to be lived out progressively. While beginning with a crisis, it is also a process in spiritual development. In the act of sanctification, nothing essentially human is removed. Rather, it is the cleansing of the inner self as we consecrate all to God. Mildred Bangs Wynkoop, in her excellent book *Foundations of Wesleyan-Arminian Theology*, speaks of the evidence of this infilling as follows:

> A heart wholly loving God—a unified personality—is the badge. No part of the human psyche can be left out. The regenerating and cleansing effects of the grace of God go at least as deep now as the "heart," out of which "come the issues of life."

> The New Testament teaches that it is the self itself that is cleansed from double-mindedness (James 1:8) and sin (1 John 1:9).[4]

All of our human emotions are left fully intact, but cleansed and sensitized by the Holy Spirit. Too long we have failed to openly acknowledge

---

[2]Dayton, "Holiness Truth in Romans," 89.

[3]Earle, "Consecration and Crucifixion," 79.

[4]Wynkoop, *Foundations of Wesleyan-Arminian Theology*, 113–114.

that a "saint" becomes angry, loves deeply, and may have a real sense of spiritual pride. But this human nature once stained by sin has been forgiven by his grace, consecrated to his will, and cleansed by his Spirit. Holiness is the way to wholeness!

FOR FURTHER STUDY:

1. What is the basis for believing in scriptural holiness?

2. Define *holiness* as it relates to the nature of God, then as it relates to human holiness.

3. What is the relationship between the biblical terms *holiness* and *sanctification*?

4. Discuss the teaching of entire sanctification. Is Paul's use of *wholly* (1 Thess 5:23, KJV) comforting or confusing? Why?

5. What is the significance of the common expression, a "second work of grace"? Consider how such an expression developed in our understanding of the ministry of the Holy Spirit.

6. Explain the involvement of the Holy Spirit in the experiences of salvation and sanctification.

7. Is Christian perfection taught in the New Testament? Consider Matthew 5:48 and 2 Corinthians 7:1.

The *Holy Ghost* shall come upon thee,
and the power of the Highest shall overshadow thee.
Therefore also that holy thing which shall be born of thee
shall be called the Son of God.

—LUKE 1:35, KJV

PRELUDE
TO
PENTECOST

*What God is determines what He does. The divine character gives
color to the divine creations. What is the keynote to the harmonies
of heaven in the heart of Deity? Holiness eternally impeccable...
the Pentecostal prelude.*

J. Paul Taylor
The Music of Pentecost, 16

4

The Prelude to Pentecost

SITTING QUIETLY in a large auditorium, I listened attentively to the prelude of the symphony. The opening strains of the music were only indicative of the major presentation to follow. But even in the prelude, all of the instruments were in tune and under the direction of the conductor, producing harmony as the musical score moved toward the major theme.

So it is as one reads the gospels of Matthew, Mark, and Luke, witnessing the ministry of the Holy Spirit. While there are only a few references to his involvement in the birth, life, death, and resurrection of Christ, they are vitally important. These references prepare us for all that is to follow. Each instance reveals that the divine conductor is directing persons who are in tune with him, yielded to his control and surrendered to his perfect will. Like a progressive revelation, each movement of the music leads us toward the spiritual harmony of Pentecost.

Preparation

According to God's divine plan, all of history moved towards the coming of Christ, the Savior of the world. Preparation had been made! Prophecy had been proclaimed, history accomplished, and individuals selected for the fulfillment of Scripture. In perfect harmony, each participant responded as directed. Zacharias the priest and Elizabeth his wife "were upright in the sight of God, observing all the Lord's commandments and regulations blamelessly" (Luke 1:6). Such surrendered persons were to share in the preparation for the coming of the Christ. Speaking to Zacharias, the angel of the Lord informed him of the coming of John the baptizer, describing him as one "filled with the *Holy Ghost*, even from his mother's womb" (Luke 1:15, KJV). Then at the birth of this forerunner of Christ, "Zacharias was filled with the *Holy Ghost,* and prophesied" (Luke 1:67, KJV). The obedience of both Zacharias and Elizabeth is indicative of the surrender always required of those who would be used of the Holy Spirit.

Complete trust, obedience, and acceptance of God's will are prerequisites to the presence of the Holy Spirit in human life. Such surrender by his parents no doubt enabled John to see that, beyond water baptism for the outward person, there was a needed cleansing of the inner person. In each of the Gospels, his words prepare us for the perfection of Pentecost: "I indeed baptize you with water unto repentance; but he that cometh after me is mightier than I, whose shoes I am not worthy to bear: he shall baptize you with the *Holy Ghost,* and with fire" (Matt 3:11, KJV; cf. Mark 1:7 and Luke 3:16–17).

Incarnation

The miracle of the incarnation is still a challenge to the minds of theologians. With our reservoir of wisdom regarding genetics and human reproduction, it is beyond some to accept the biblical account of the virgin birth. One's belief in the power and person of the Holy Spirit is tested at this point. Does the Holy Spirit perform miracles? Is he able to go beyond the human in bringing God's will to pass?

To Mary, there was no questioning once God had given the explanation of his plan. Living in anticipation of her marriage to Joseph, having never known a man intimately, she was astounded when informed that she would bear a child. In response to this, the angel of the Lord said: "The *Holy Ghost* shall come upon thee, and the power of the Highest shall overshadow thee. Therefore also that holy thing which shall be born of thee shall be called the Son of God" (Luke 1:35, KJV; see also Matt 1:18).

Once again the fears of Mary and Joseph were allayed because of their attitude toward the will of God. Joseph, seeking to treat his bride-to-be in the proper manner and to avoid embarrassment, was reassured by the angels that the miracle of the incarnation was wrought by the Holy Ghost (Matt 1:20–21).

How wonderful that even today the Holy Spirit indwells the lives of people surrendered to God's will! The incarnation speaks of God's desire to clothe himself in humanity, thus revealing himself and his love to the world. Through the presence of the Holy Spirit abiding in the lives of persons like yourself, God has a new incarnation.

Authentication

God's plan, anticipated and incarnate, now needed to be validated to show the fulfillment of prophecy. As the prelude moves toward the major theme of the music, so the Holy Spirit authenticates all that has come to pass.

John, baptizing near the Jordan river, is confronted by Christ, who presents himself to be baptized. Recognizing the "Lamb of God," John demonstrates the humility of a surrendered life, asking to be baptized of Jesus. Yet Jesus encourages John to proceed. He does baptize the Christ, and the Holy Spirit authenticates this act. "As soon as Jesus was baptized, he went up out of the water. At that moment heaven was opened, and he saw the Spirit of God descending like a dove and lighting on him. And a voice from heaven said, 'This is my Son, whom I love; with him I am well pleased'" (Matt 3:16–17). Some writers have noted that in this act all three persons of the Trinity are active: *Christ* in presentation, the *Holy Spirit* as the dove in affirmation, and the voice of *God* in confirmation.

Having received this divine approval at such a public gathering, Jesus is then "led by the Spirit into the desert to be tempted by the devil" (Matt 4:1; cf. Mark 1:12 and Luke 4:1). If his ministry was to be helpful to sinful humanity, it was necessary that he be "tempted in every way, just as we are—yet was without sin" (Heb 4:15). Thus, where the battles of the soul are waged (many times over very legitimate appetites, like the hunger for food), Jesus was led by the Spirit. We should remember that life in the Spirit is not always one of ease, free of temptation. Rather, such commitment on the part of the Christian may precipitate the greater struggle of the soul—a struggle through which we may come victoriously when we rely, as did Christ, on the Word of God as our strength.

With public approval through baptism, and personal affirmation through victory in the wilderness, Jesus now prepares for his ministry to people. To do so required more than innate abilities, equipping him to relate to people, or the ability to speak well from the prophets. Something above and beyond all of this had to be present. Luke 4:18 speaks of the prophecy of Isaiah: "The Spirit of the Sovereign LORD is on me, because the LORD has anointed me to preach good news to the poor. He has sent me to bind up the brokenhearted, to proclaim freedom for the captives and release from darkness for the prisoners, to proclaim the year of the LORD's favor and the day of vengeance of our God, to comfort all who mourn" (Isa 61:1–2).

God's Holy Spirit still authenticates the life and ministry of all who would serve him. To attempt to minister without the approval of the Holy

Spirit is to speak without authority. It is to testify without the experience and to speak of fullness when inwardly we are empty. He alone authenticates our ministry. "No man, not even the Son of God, can do God's work without God's spirit."[1] No gift or ability equips us for service in the body of Christ other than the Holy Spirit. All who would serve as laborers in the vineyard of the Lord—educators, musicians, administrators, preachers, missionaries, and all other servants—must be filled with the Holy Spirit and approved by him.

Continuation

Entering into his ministry, approved and anointed by the Holy Spirit, Jesus established a pattern for the people of God. Here in the formative stages of the church, Jesus was putting into practice those things that would guide us across the centuries. That which lasts is not that which we have devised and developed in our own doing; rather, the lasting ministry is that which is given by the Holy Spirit. Will what we are doing continue after we are gone? How long will this message of truth continue?

Each writer in the Synoptic Gospels picks up the same inspiration for testing the lasting quality of this truth. Mark 13:11 is an example of the continuing inspiration that comes through surrender to the Spirit of God: "But when they shall lead you, and deliver you up, take no thought beforehand what ye shall speak, neither do ye premeditate: but whatsoever shall be given you in that hour, that speak ye: for it is not ye that speak, but the Holy Ghost" (KJV; cf. Matt 10:20 and Luke 12:12).

Fully aware that persecution would come upon those who would live godly in this world, Jesus gave the assurance of God's continuing guidance and presence. The same Spirit that fulfilled prophecy, that brought Christ into the world and validated his ministry—this blessed Holy Spirit will be with you to accomplish God's purpose in your life. Trust him; allow him to possess and fill you. He will not fail! With this prelude, your spiritual life can become a symphony under the direction of God.

FOR FURTHER STUDY:

1. What common characteristics are to be found in the people chosen by God to be used of the Holy Spirit? Examples: Elizabeth, Mary, John the baptizer.

---

[1]Barclay, *Promise of the Spirit*, 23.

2. Discover other scriptural passages regarding the doctrine of the incarnation. List the passages and seek to relate them to the verses mentioned in this chapter.

3. What are the qualities of a spiritual life that give authenticity to one's ministry? Are such qualities humanly developed or divinely endowed?

4. Is it possible for one to be filled with the Holy Spirit and fail to progress? Give reasoning for your response.

5. Are there dangers in making all the ministry of the Holy Spirit post-Pentecost? If so, please list the inherent dangers to such teaching.

6. Does the obedient Christian possess full power when filled with the Spirit, or should a continuation in the Spirit-filled life produce greater strengths?

7. Does the harmony of the Pentecostal experience mean that life will have no sour notes? If not, then what does the term *harmony* mean?

If you love me, you will obey what I command.
And I will ask my Father,
and he will give you another *Counselor*
to be with you forever—the Spirit of truth.

—JOHN 14:15–17

A
COUNSELOR
FOR YOU

*If we would walk in the Spirit we must trust Him and count upon Him
in the emergencies of life. We must regard Him as our* Counselor *who
has undertaken our cause and expects to be called upon in every time
of need, one who will unfailingly be found faithful and all-sufficient in
every crisis.*

A. B. Simpson
The Gentle Love of the Holy Spirit, 15
(emphasis added)

5

A Counselor for You

LIKE WATER to a thirsty pilgrim is the gospel of John in our quest for the Holy Spirit. The insatiable desire to know him and to experience his fullness finds a sense of satisfaction in the knowledge of what Jesus taught about him. He alone could speak to the sufficiency of the Spirit in the meeting all of our needs, for the Holy Spirit is like unto Christ (Rom 8:9). Jesus alludes to this living water: "'If anyone is thirsty, let him come to me and drink. Whoever believes in me, as the Scripture has said, streams of living water will flow from within him.' By this he meant the Spirit, whom those who believed in him were later to receive. Up to that time the Spirit had not been given, since Jesus had not yet been glorified." (John 7:37–39).

Having spoken of this adequacy to satisfy the soul, John hurries on to remind us that the Holy Spirit had not yet been given in his fullness. However, he points to the time when Christ would be glorified and Pentecost would become a reality for all who believe. It is because of this that we find in this gospel the most influential source of material regarding the Holy Spirit.

While the Holy Spirit is recognized as an active participant in the work of regeneration (John 3:5–8), the major body of John's material about the Spirit is found in chapters 14, 15, and 16. These passages center around the last days of Christ's earthly ministry. His followers —not fully grasping all of his teachings, unwilling to turn loose of him—face the possibility of disillusionment, discouragement, and despair. For three years they have had a companion, counselor, and guide in whom they could trust. Now Jesus counsels them about the future

51

and his provision for their continued home through the ministry of the Holy Spirit.

His Comforting Assurance

Once again the word used to describe the Spirit is of importance to the student of Scripture. As noted in previous chapters, the Old Testament writers spoke of *ruach*, "the breath of God." In the Synoptic Gospels and many of the Epistles, the word *pneuma* refers to the "wind of God." But now, in an attempt to convey to the followers of Christ the full intent of Jesus' concern, John brings into use the Greek word *paraclete*. While translated in the King James Version as "comforter," the word has a much greater meaning. It was the intent of Jesus that the disciples would be sustained by the promise of the Comforter during this time of transition between the resurrection and Pentecost. His assurance is comforting to all humanity as we capture a glimpse of the intent of Christ, our Lord: "I will pray the Father, and he shall give you another Comforter, that he may abide with you forever; Even the Spirit of Truth, whom the world cannot receive, because it seeth him not, neither knoweth him: but ye know him; for he dwelleth with you, and shall be in you. I will not leave you comfortless: I will come to you" (John 14:16–18, KJV).

This is no security blanket for the saints. He assures his followers of the indwelling presence of the Holy Spirit in their lives. While in a measure the Spirit had been *with* them, here was the assurance that he would be *in* them. Jesus gave his word that this Comforter would become for them the "wonderful Counselor" of Isaiah. As such, he would intercede for them and become their helper in times of weakness, one to walk beside them no matter how difficult the situation or circumstance.

This kind of assurance was built upon the possibilities of Pentecost. It was God's revelation through the Son, of provision made for all who would follow "the way and the truth and the life" (John 14:6). In Jesus' high priestly prayer in John 17, the far-reaching effects of this truth touches our lives today: "My prayer is not for them alone. I pray also for *those who will believe in me* through their message" (17:20). Reaching across the ages, Jesus gives to us the comforting assurance of the divine adequacy of the Spirit-filled life. No sorrow is too severe, no tragedy too terrible but that the Holy Spirit can make us "more than conquerors" (Rom 8:37).

His Continuing Presence

Words of assurance must always be supported by the awareness of God's divine presence with you. Therefore, John's writing clearly indicates by direct statement or implication that this presence will be within the obedient believer.

As Jesus prayed for the comforting assurance of the Holy Spirit, his words were "that he may *abide* with you for ever" (14:16, KJV). In the discourse about the true vine, he indicates that our life sustenance and accessibility to the resources of God are dependent upon this continuing relationship. "If ye *abide* in me, and my words *abide* in you, ye shall ask what ye will, and it shall be done unto you" (15:7, KJV). While the word *abide* is not used in John 17, it is implied in the meaning of Jesus' words: "that they all may be one; as thou, Father, art in me, and I in thee, that they also may be one in us" (17:21, KJV).

While limited by his earthly body, it was not possible for the Christ to be in every place all the time. In reality, to be *with* them and *in* them permanently, it was necessary for him to leave them temporarily. Only through the coming of the Holy Spirit would he be able to "abide" with them; for that reason, it was expedient or necessary that he return to the Father. Essential to the relationship of his continuing presence is the requirement that we "abide" in him. The emphasis placed upon love and obedience cannot be overlooked in this context. "If ye love me, keep my commandments" (14:15, KJV) and "If ye keep my commandments, ye shall abide in my love" (15:10, KJV) are both indicative of the Spirit-filled life. The abiding presence of the Holy Spirit within us will be obvious by the witness of our lives as we abide in him.

Herein was the stabilizing influence of the Spirit. Rather than an experience based on emotional feelings, it is the strong assurance that you are abiding in God's love, obedient to his Word. Because of this, the Holy Spirit abides within your own life. A life of ethical and moral holiness is a natural outgrowth of this experience of constantly "abiding." A total life of unity through the Holy Spirit is God's plan for the church.

His Calling to Remembrance

Jesus knew what was in us, our strengths and our weaknesses. Therefore, he was concerned lest we forget, or fail to comprehend, all that he had taught. To assist us in remembering, the Holy Spirit becomes our teacher, calling to mind the teachings of Christ and his Word: "But the Comforter, which is the Holy Ghost, whom the Father will send in my name, he shall teach you all things, and bring all things to your remembrance, whatsoever I have said unto you" (John 14:26, KJV).

Spiritual restlessness is often the result of failing to respond to, or to remember, Jesus' words. It is not by accident that the verse on peace immediately follows the above-mentioned passage. Divine peace is based upon knowing and doing the will of God. Truth is never destroyed, but oft times it has been pushed aside to be forgotten or ignored. Some truth has never been rightly understood due to our human limitations. Because of this, Jesus wants to give the Holy Spirit as a teacher to enable us to understand and to remember the truth that he taught.

"All truth," as mentioned in John 16:13, is not to be misconstrued to claim for ourselves a superior knowledge or exclusive right to doctrine. The "truth" refers primarily to the redemptive life, death, and resurrection of Christ. This teacher within in no way relieves the child of God of the need to study to show oneself approved unto God as one who rightly divides the word of truth (2 Tim 2:15). It only places upon us the greater responsibility because we have had the opportunity of being under the tutelage of the Holy Spirit, who enables us to assimilate truth into our lives. Such a relationship with the teacher of truth leaves no room for the attitude that we have received all the truth. In the heart where the Spirit rules, there is always a humble attitude of desiring to know more of God's will.

His Convicting Influence

While assuring the disciples of the Holy Spirit's presence for their continued growth in holiness, Jesus also speaks of his influence in the world. "And when he is come, he will reprove the world of sin, and of righteousness, and of judgment" (John 16:8). While the King James Version and the New International Version use the word *reprove,* the American Standard Version and the Weymouth translation use the word *convince,* meaning to awaken to a sense of sin, or to unmask one's sin. Such a ministry has been performed by the Holy Spirit through his influence in the world following the day of Pentecost.

To a disbelieving world, there is nothing more disturbing or convincing than people surrendered to and possessed by the Holy Spirit. His very presence within the obedient life produces a holiness that confronts sinful people with their failures, thus becoming a disturbing influence. It is equally true that the most convincing evidence of the sanctifying experience is a life of holiness—a life that has recognized sin for what it is, has turned to righteousness through repentance, and now lives in the constant awareness of the judgment to come. Only such lives, convicted and convinced by the Holy Spirit, lend credence to our theology of the Holy Spirit. His love in the heart of the sanctified brings conviction to a disbelieving, Christ-rejecting world, awakening in them the desire for holiness of heart and life. His counsel makes us to know that there is a divine plus to the experience of Pentecost; it is a positive, not a negative.

In an age when we are tempted toward manipulation and exploitation through the use of advertising gimmicks and modern technology, we would do well to read this passage of Scripture often. Conviction is the work of the Holy Spirit. It is not mood-setting music, soft lighting effects, and spiritual showmanship in the pulpit. Such antics may create an emotional stir that will bring a response for the moment, but they will not be able to stand the test of time. Conviction is the work of the Holy Spirit in the hearts of those who will heed his call. He may work through the life of the weakest or strongest vessel; but if lasting good is produced, it will be the result of the convincing influence of the Spirit of God. It is the kind of influence we desire and seek through our divine Counselor.

For further study:

1. Explain the use of the term *Comforter* (kjv) in our understanding of the Holy Spirit as spoken of in John 14:15–18.

2. Discuss the evidence of the abiding presence of the Holy Spirit in the individual life. Is this evidence merely a refined human nature, or is there a divine/human interaction that makes it possible?

3. As Counselor, the Spirit seeks to guide us into "all truth." What does this say with regard to the person who never comes to any new truth or spiritual growth?

4. Evaluate the use of different techniques in seeking to produce conviction in the life of the unbeliever. How can one know when conviction is of the Holy Spirit?

5. How does one remain sensitive to the counsel and leadership of the Holy Spirit? When is one most receptive to his leadership?

6. If the Holy Spirit convicts the world of sin, why is it that there is such a difference in interpretation as to what sin is? Is there a distinction to be made between *sin* and *sins*?

And behold, I send the *promise of my Father* upon you:
but tarry ye in the city of Jerusalem,
until ye be endued with power from on high.

—LUKE 24:49, KJV

THE PROMISE
OF THE
FATHER

The "promise of the Father" was the promise of the Spirit dwelling within persons. Saints in the New Testament are thus those who are made holy by the indwelling Spirit. The "promise of the Father" thus inaugurated Christ's reign in the hearts of believers.

Laurence W. Wood
Pentecostal Grace, 38
(emphasis added)

6

The Promise of the Father

GOD'S PROMISES never fail! Though not always fulfilled when we would like, the plan of God moves on inevitably toward his perfect goal. Israel, God's people, had discovered the reliability of these promises. In community celebrations, their history always recounted these blessings as the fulfillment of God's promise. "I declare today to the LORD your God that I have come to the land the LORD swore to our forefathers to give us" (Deut 26:3; see also vv. 1–10).

God had promised them a land of milk and honey, a Messiah, and a life of abundance. Through all of their wilderness wanderings, they continued to hold onto these precious promises from the past, believing at times against insurmountable obstacles. The promise lured them on. Jesus, resurrected from Joseph's borrowed tomb and endeavoring to prepare the disciples for his ascension, reminds them once again of the "promise of the Father" (Luke 24:49, KJV). Here was a link with their history and a foundation for their faith in the future. While God had made the promise to their ancestors and Christ had become the embodiment of that promise in the flesh, now God's promise of the Spirit would be poured out on them, to dwell in them. When such a reminder was given by Christ, at least three things took place. The promise of the Father made them *realize* the validity of their past, it enabled them to *visualize* the possibilities of their future, and it allowed them to *actualize* the reality of the present experience. Let us look at God's promise to us in this same context.

Realize

In the Old Testament teachings of the Holy Spirit, there are at least three passages that the people of God would have related to this statement of Jesus regarding the promise of the Father. Found in the writings of Isaiah, Ezekiel, and Joel, they focus our attention on that to which Jesus pointed. Certain truths surface in each passage that are important to our understanding of the Spirit-filled life. First, each promises the coming of God's Spirit upon his people. Second, each promises that the Spirit will be given in abundance, liberally poured out upon them. And finally, each promises that the Spirit will make them productive, growing in godliness and for his glory. These same promises are given to us and may be realized through the Holy Spirit in this very hour:

> This is what the LORD says—he who made you, who formed you in the womb, and who will help you: Do not be afraid, O Jacob, my servant, Jeshurun, whom I have chosen. For I will pour water on the thirsty land, and streams on the dry ground; I will *pour out my Spirit* on your offspring, and my blessing on your descendants. They will spring up like grass in a meadow, like poplar trees by flowing streams (Isa 44:2–4).

> Then they will know that I am the LORD their God, for though I sent them into exile among the nations, I will gather them to their own land, not leaving any behind. I will no longer hide my face from them, for I will *pour out my Spirit* on the house of Israel, declares the Sovereign LORD (Ezek 39:28–29).

> And afterward, I will pour out my Spirit on all people. Your sons and daughters will prophesy, your old men will dream dreams, your young men will see visions. Even on my servants, both men and women, I will *pour out my Spirit* in those days (Joel 2:28–29).

Only against Israel's background of nomadic wanderings and struggles can the richness of the Father's promise be fully understood. As the patriarch of old would bless the oldest son, pouring out his inheritance upon him, so Israel longed for this outpouring of God's Spirit upon them. Having faced the barren wilderness without sufficient water to produce vegetation, they were captivated by visions of springs of living water poured out on the dry ground. With this promise before them, their hopes were kept alive—even during the silent years following the prophecy of Malachi—as they awaited the coming of their Messiah. Now this resurrected Lord stands before them, helping them to realize once again the validity of these ancient prophecies.

The promise of the Father is just before you. Don't become impatient. Wait! God will validate his promise to you.

Visualize

In calling to remembrance the promises of God, Jesus also helped the disciples to visualize the possibilities of the future. The words of Jesus found in Luke 24:49 and Acts 1:4–5 place a command upon his followers. They are to "tarry" or "wait" for the promise of the Father. Only then do dreams and visions become a possibility. Though they had received the divine commission to go into all the world, preaching and teaching the gospel, the success of their work was contingent on their obediently waiting to receive the Spirit's infilling. Without him, they could do nothing but fail. With him, nothing they did could fail. They could hardly visualize what would happen during the first century of the young church. Signs and wonders followed them. The sick were healed, prison doors were opened, social and cultural barriers were broken down, devils were cast out, and people were saved by the thousands. The Scriptures speak of the early Christians turning their world upside down (Acts 17:6).

It was beyond their fondest dreams, but it was exactly what the Father had promised. Upon these barren, unproductive lives, God would pour out his Spirit, making them productive, fruit-bearing Christians. Joel had been right when prophesying, "Your old men will dream dreams, your young men will see visions" (2:28).

Without question, we too need to be reminded of the Father's promise so that we might visualize the future for the church. When some speak of a post-Christian era and others refer to the church's having lost her relevance in this age, we need to capture a vision of what the Father's promise can mean today. "Where there is no vision the people perish" (Prov 29:18, KJV). The Kingdom has come! The church is alive and well! And under the leadership of the Holy Spirit, it marches as a mighty, victorious army.

Actualize

Past prophecy and future possibility mean little unless there is a present reality. Therefore, the promise of the Father—the promise for which they were waiting in the upper room—must be actualized. To be authentic, it would be necessary to fulfill the three thoughts common in the passages of Isaiah, Ezekiel, and Joel. However, the Holy Spirit could not—yea, would not—come until proper readiness had been made. Therefore, we should note the setting for this inauguration of the church.

In obedience to the command of Christ to wait for the promise of the Father, 120 believers gathered in the upper room (Acts 1:13–15). We do well to recognize that not every believer was there for this Pentecostal outpouring. Paul tells us that about five hundred of the brethren saw the risen Christ (1 Cor 15:6); but in the Acts account of the Pentecostal experience, only 120 were in attendance. Not everyone receives the fullness of the Holy Spirit at the same time or in the same way. But it is evident from the account that certain conditions must be met.

First, the giving of the Holy Spirit was at God's time and not the believers'. "When the day of Pentecost came" (Acts 2:1), divinity had priority! The Holy Spirit never comes where there is competition or where he takes second place. Only through unconditional surrender of the human will, does the divine Spirit enter the heart.

Second, Pentecost can only come when unity prevails. "They were all with one accord in one place" (2:1, KJV). Human will had been crucified; jealous competition confessed and forgiven; hurt feelings healed and resentment removed. One great desire possessed all who met in that upper room: the desire to be filled with the Holy Spirit, the promise of the Father.

When such conditions are met, God always keeps his promise. There is not a broken life anywhere that God would not bless with his Spirit if the individual will only come to the place of total surrender to God. There is not a congregation anywhere, of any size—no matter what difficulties it may be facing—that cannot receive new life if it will but realize the promise of the Father, visualize the possibilities, and then *actualize*, really experience, Pentecost.

God will give your congregation new life and growth. Just as Peter said, "This is what was spoken by the prophet Joel" (Acts 2:16). God has promised, and he will not fail.

For further study:

1. What are the common passages from the Old Testament that deal with the "promise of the Father"? Study them in their full scriptural context and discover implications for our study of the Holy Spirit.

2. What are other promises in God's Word that the believer may claim regarding the Holy Spirit?

3. Is it possible for one to be a Christian and not receive the "promise of the Father" regarding the Holy Spirit?

4. Is this promise limited to only certain persons? If so, who are they and what are the qualifying factors involved?

5. Compare the prophetic statement of Joel 2:28–29 with the fulfillment in Acts 2:1–4. Do you see in this the keeping of God's promise?

6. In what way is the promise of power through the Holy Spirit manifest in the world today?

But the *fruit of the Spirit*
is love,

joy,

peace

—GALATIANS 5:22

HIS SPIRIT
IN MY
PERSONALITY

The phrase "fruit of the Spirit" *assigns the graces of the Christian character to their proper source. They are not of man's producing. They do not spring from the soil of the carnal nature. Men do not gather grapes of thorns, or figs of thistles.*

Samuel Chadwick
The Way to Pentecost, 88
(emphasis added)

7

His Spirit in My Personality

LIFE IN THE SPIRIT is productive! This promise actualized on the day of Pentecost now begins to bear the fruit of the Spirit. While the Pauline letters speak of both the "fruit" and the "gifts" of the Spirit, we will give priority to the "fruit" that is produced in the Spirit-filled life. Although the word *fruit* is in the singular, it refers to a cluster of Christian characteristics or graces. Paul's intent is to emphasize that all of these are produced through the Holy Spirit's enduement of divine love. He begins his list of the fruit of the Spirit with love. He admonishes the church that, when speaking of gifts, they should seek "the most excellent way," which is God's way of love (1 Cor 12:31). In his study of life in the Spirit, Samuel Chadwick places emphasis on the difference between "gifts" and "fruit," stressing that gifts often are works of the flesh. Yet the fruit of the Christian life is always produced through our relationship to Christ as his Spirit abides in us (John 15). Scripture is very plain in stating that fruit is the expected result of every believer; but there is no such concept regarding gifts. God gives the gifts "as he determines" (1 Cor 12:11), implying that some may not be so endued. The fruit listed in Galatians is not physical but attitudinal, dealing with that which is within us.

The obvious transformation of human personalities through the Holy Spirit is shown by the disciples in Acts 2:14. We immediately recognize that their attitudes of self-seeking for the choice seats in the Kingdom had been changed. Rather than competing, their main concern now was to demonstrate the unity of the Spirit of Christ. Further evidence is given in verses 41 through 47, where we recognize the disciples' harmonious concern for the work of God, their unselfish giving of possessions, their joyful spirit, and their relationship to other people. Already the fruit of the Holy Spirit was being produced. The fruit of these early Christians were not only spiritual; they were practical and livable.

Such sanctified living stands in vivid contrast to the world, the flesh, and the devil. In his Magna Carta of Christian liberty recorded in Galatians, Paul uses this contrast to emphasize the fruit of the Spirit-filled life. After dealing with the concept of being set free from sin by the blood of Christ (Gal 5:1), he seeks to help them in the continuing struggle between the "flesh" and the "Spirit." It is the fruit of the Spirit in the Christian life that enables one to triumph over the fleshly attitudes and appetites that confront us continually. No, being filled with the Spirit does not eliminate the possibility of being tempted. But as we allow the Holy Spirit to possess our personalities, he can give us victory over the temptations of the flesh.

Both the works of the flesh and the fruit of the Spirit can be divided into threes, a triad that is common in many scriptural studies. View them side-by-side in Galatians 5:19–23. It may be helpful in gaining a clear perspective as to the pervasive nature of the Holy Spirit in the individual personality.

We recognize from this comparison that the fruit of the Spirit enables us to deal with personal areas of need. Areas that deal with person-to-God relationships, person-to-person relationships, and one's relationship with one's self. For our study, I have used the terms *personality, relationship,* and *discipline.* In this chapter, we speak of the Holy Spirit's producing in us that fruit which comes from the person-to-God relationship.

Love

When Paul uses the word *love,* he is not referring to the term as it is usually understood in today's society. In this hour of history, the word may express almost anything from the ludicrous to the laudable. But as used in the context of Galatians 5:22, it carries a much more profound meaning. To the Greek, four words were used to convey the various meanings of love. *Eros* was the love of man and woman, a physical relationship. It is the word from which we derive *erotic.* The highest type of human love was expressed by the word *philia* and referred to a lasting friendship, a kind of brotherly love. The parent-child relationship was known as *storge,* the love of one's own family. While all of these terms expressed love in varied relationships, Paul sought a word that would convey love at its ultimate, and that word was *agape.*[1] This love is more than physical attraction,

---

[1] For a more complete study of the New Testament words for love, see Barclay, *More New Testament Words,* 11–24.

Works of the Flesh Galatians 5:19–21	Fruit of the Spirit[2] Galatians 5:22–23
1. *Sins against God's commandments:* —impure thoughts —eagerness for lustful pleasure —idolatry —spiritism	1. *God-ward relationship:* —love: God's agape —joy: love's cheerfulness —peace: love's confidence

2. *Sins expressed against other people:*
—hatred and fighting
—jealousy and anger
—complaints and criticism
—group superiority
—wrong doctrine
—envy and murder
	2. *Man-ward relationships:*
	—longsuffering (patience):
	  love's composure
	  patience under trial
	—gentleness (kindness):
	  love's consideration
	  kindly disposed to others
	—goodness:
	  love's character
	  beneficence, kindness in action

3. *Sins against one's self:*
—drunkenness
—revellings (wild parties)
	3. *Self-ward relationship:*
	—faith (faithfulness):
	  love's constancy
	  fidelity, trustworthiness
	—meekness (gentleness):
	  love's humility
	  mildness and submissiveness
	—temperance (self-control):
	  love's conquest

[2]Various combinations and divisions of these are found in several writings. The author has selected these to help the reader capture a few of the graces ministering to the three relationships indicated.

family devotion, or brotherly concern. It is love born of God and revealed in Christ. More than emotional feeling, this love finds expression in doing unto others for their own personal good.

To know that "God is love" is to understand our dependence upon the Spirit to reproduce this quality in our personalities. *Agape* love is not a character trait that one develops by taking a course in understanding human nature. It is an experience that finds expression through growth in Christ—the Holy Spirit enabling us to love as he loved.

The covenant-love (Hebrew *chesed*) and election-love (Hebrew *ahabah*) of the Old Testament[3] find fulfillment in this New Testament word, *agape*. All of the steadfast faithfulness of God, the "ties of love" (Hos 11:4), are now amplified in this Pauline concept of what God's love is like. Such love wills to love, even when we are unlovely. It does not count the cost when seeking the good of another. Basically, *agape* love is the active determination of the will.

John said, "God so loved...that he gave..." (3:16). There was no other reason! No one made him do it. He did it because of his love for lost humanity. And Paul portrays this continuing concern of God for us in Romans 5:8: "But God demonstrates his own love for us in this: While we were still sinners, Christ died for us." This kind of love is not just a good feeling; it is the fruit of the Holy Spirit, who enables us to be "patient and kind, never jealous or envious, never boastful or proud, never haughty or selfish or rude. Love does not demand its own way. It is not irritable or touchy. It does not hold grudges and will hardly even notice when others do it wrong" (1 Cor 13:4–5, LB). In light of this passage, one understands the term most often used by John Wesley, "perfect love." Certainly such qualities demand a divine infilling if they are to be reproduced in our personalities. This comes only through the Holy Ghost. "The love of God is shed abroad in our hearts by the Holy Ghost which is given unto us" (Rom 5:5, KJV). It is not a disposition that comes gradually through mellowing with the years. Rather, it is the refreshing love of eternal youthfulness motivating us to strive for the most noble ideals, willing to risk all in their achievement.

Just as Jesus sacrificially gave himself for us, we in response give ourselves in sacrificial love and service to him. And as God's love overcame all obstacles and outlasts all else, so this fruit of the Spirit will continue to

---

[3]For a more complete study of this Old Testament concept of love, see Snaith, *Distinctive Ideas of the Old Testament*, 94–142.

be productive. For "now these three remain: faith, hope and love. But the greatest of these is love" (1 Cor 13:13).

Joy

Joy is the emotional expression of love. From the angelic annunciation of Christ's advent into history until the conclusion of the book of Revelation, an unending joy pervades the Scriptures. In the Gospels, it is "good news of great joy" (Luke 2:10), and in the consummation of human history, it is the joyous victory of those who have overcome and in jubilation make the courts of heaven ring (Rev 12:11). Joy is the atmosphere of the New Testament. It is the radiant expression of the nature of Christ. Even in the midst of the most adverse circumstances, the excruciating, humiliating pain of the cross, our Lord was able to experience this inner joy. The writer of Hebrews states, "For the joy set before him [Christ] endured the cross" (12:2). This is joy produced by the awareness that, no matter how unpleasant the surroundings or how severe the sufferings, God's love is more than adequate. It is the enabling presence of the Holy Spirit that allows us to be joyful in unpleasant situations.

Although the Philippian letter is one of joy, the experiences of Paul and Silas in that community were not always pleasant. On one occasion, they were thrown into jail, placed in stocks, and left unattended. But there in the midnight darkness, they began to sing and praise the Lord (Acts 16:25). There is only one explanation for such spiritual ecstasy: They had the indwelling source of joy, which was not dependent on emotional or physical feelings. Theirs was the fruit of the Spirit—joy produced because of his presence. Because of this, Paul could describe the early Christians as those who were "sorrowful, yet always rejoicing" (2 Cor 6:10).

Peace

God's love produces personal peace—peace that is expressed even in the midst of conflict. The true peace revealed in God's Word is not simply the absence of frustration, faults, and failures. It is not the state of being freed from all anxieties and worries. Rather, it is produced by the presence of the Holy Spirit abiding as the dove of peace. It is a peace that comes only when we cease striving to be righteous in our own human goodness and allow the Prince of Peace to possess us completely. He has become our example of peace as he triumphed over tension and trials, remained calm in conflict, and surrendered to suffering without defeat. Remember, it was to disillusioned and discouraged disciples that Jesus said, "Peace I leave with you; my peace I give you" (John 14:27). Here was the peace that prevailed in persecution and enabled the early Christians to change their culture.

Such peace must always begin, as we have indicated, by first making peace *with* God through the experience of spiritual rebirth. This right relationship with him removes the conflict of contending loyalties. Now we have peace *with* God. This knowledge within allows us the joyful experience of letting the Holy Spirit produce in us the peace *of* God. It is the peace *of* God that continues as he controls our lives. "You will keep in perfect peace him whose mind is steadfast, because he trusts in you" (Isa 26:3). The free person in Christ has made a decision to become a love-slave to the Lord, who is the peace-giver. This, and this alone, can produce in the human personality the "peace which transcends all understanding" (Phil 4:7).

FOR FURTHER STUDY:

1. Why does the author give priority to the "fruit" of the Spirit rather than to the "gifts"?

2. Where does the primary work of the Holy Spirit take place in the individual's life? Is it internal or external? Explain your response.

3. In seeking to have the Spirit in your personality, how do you maintain proper motives for doing so? Is it possible to seek him selfishly?

4. Is it possible to love God completely and still love family and friends as one should?

5. How does one reconcile the biblical pattern of perfect love with the fact that some people claim to be incompatible? Can one love perfectly and still not be able to relate to others properly?

6. How is the joy of the Spirit-filled life different from the pleasure that the world gives?

7. Please distinguish between the peace of God and the peace of apathy that sometimes reveals itself among church people. How do we differentiate the two?

The *fruit of the Spirit* is…
longsuffering,
gentleness,
goodness….

—GALATIANS 5:22, KJV

HIS SPIRIT
IN
MY RELATIONSHIPS

The fruit of the Spirit *begins with the characteristics of the spiritual mind and passes on to its manifestations in personal character, social virtues, and practical conduct…*

…[Fruit] *refers to character, and sets forth the kind of man the Spirit produces rather than the things He inspires him to do.*

Samuel Chadwick
The Way to Pentecost, 88, 90
(emphasis added)*

---

*The use of "man" and "him" in no way restricts Chadwick's observations to men only; this passage should be understood to apply to both men and women.

8

His Spirit in My Relationships

SEEKING TO KNOW God in a personal, intimate relationship prepares the soil of the soul to produce the fruit of the Spirit. Such a relationship with God must always eventuate in right relationship with one's neighbor or it contradicts the Christian faith. The first and greatest commandment, Jesus said, was to love the Lord with your total personality—all your heart, soul, and mind. But the second greatest commandment is like it: "Love your neighbor as yourself" (Matt 22:37–39). Right relationship with others can only be experienced when we have rightly related ourselves to God.

This priority was highlighted by the great Danish thinker Søren Kierkegaard in his dictum "Purity of heart is to will one thing." Until we have come to a place of commitment to Christ and his will, we remain "double-minded" persons (James 1:8). It is difficult to live with ourselves, much less get along with other people. But when Christ has come to us with forgiveness and acceptance, the inner chaos has been calmed by his "Peace be still!" Then, as we allow his Holy Spirit to dwell within us, willing with him one will, we begin to relate rightly with others around us. Ephesians 5 begins by describing this kind of relationship (vv. 1–2). Paul also alludes to the fruit of the Spirit (v. 9), then admonishes the reader to "be filled with the Spirit" (v. 18). The remaining verses of this chapter and the opening of chapter 6 deal with human relationships. Paul speaks of husbands and wives, Christ and the church, parents and children, and servants and masters.

From such clear statements about how we should live together in the body of Christ, some people might conclude that if there is any conflict, we are not living in the Spirit. But before you become disillusioned with this Spirit-filled life, remember that even entire sanctification is no guarantee that you will always agree with your brothers and sisters in Christ. Yes, at times you will even have strong disagreements with brothers and sisters in your own home.

Perhaps we should read again the account of Paul and Barnabas when they disagreed over their young missionary companion, John Mark (Acts 15:39). Each man, filled with the Holy Spirit, contended strongly for his own personal conviction—and neither gave in. Rather, each chose to go his own way, and thus was born the missionary team of Paul and Silas. We should note that as they did so, a Christian spirit prevailed.

We should also recall the serious conflict between Peter and Paul when the missionary ambassador rebuked Peter "because he was clearly in the wrong" (Gal 2:11). Paul must have believed in the value of creative conflict. God had placed in his heart the kind of divine love that allowed him to disagree strongly with other people and yet maintain a good relationship with them. David Augsburger, in his little book *The Love Fight*, reminds us that "conflict is neither good nor bad, right nor wrong. Conflict simply is. How we view, approach and work through our differences does—to a large extent—determine our whole life pattern."[1]

Remember your priority list: Love God completely with your total personality, yielding yourself to the infilling of his Holy Spirit. Then, after being able to accept yourself "in the Beloved" or "in Christ," you will discover how to love and accept your neighbor even as Christ has accepted you.

This implies that even when we were irritable, abrasive, and extremely difficult, Christ still loved us. This truth speaks to our relationships with those about us. All of us have those individual traits that are difficult for others to accept—even among pastors and parishioners, parents and children, husbands and wives. Some may want to say, "When I was filled with the Holy Spirit, all that was removed." But it is much healthier—spiritually and emotionally—to recognize these relational conflicts honestly than to attempt to camouflage them with Christian piety. The Holy Spirit will give us victory, but only as we deal with such conflict honestly rather than ignore it and hope that it will eventually go away. Let us look at some of the areas where relational problems can develop.

The simple statement that "we are all different" is a good place to begin. Few people within the Christian community would desire for everyone

---

[1]Augsburger, *Love Fight*, 3.

to be exactly alike—carbon-copy Christians or rubber-stamp saints. We believe that Christ has saved us individually and has given to us glorious freedom. However, there is a tendency to want all holiness people to be alike in outward appearance and inner experience. Because of this tendency, some of us attempt to squeeze other Christians into our own predetermined mold of what the Spirit-filled life should be. For years, I seriously questioned my own personal experience of the Holy Spirit because there were others in the community of faith who said, "When you are really filled with the Spirit you will do this…or be like this." They wanted me to be like others, more mature persons, in the church. It was therefore very helpful to me when I came across a book by William S. Deal, in which he said,

> As there are no two human beings physically and emotionally alike, so there are no two Christian experiences alike. There are similarities in all persons which identify them as members of a certain family or race, and there are likewise similarities in the Christian experiences of regeneration and sanctification by which they may be identified. There is an overall pattern which is always consistent in the experiences of all Spirit filled believers, but there is no uniformity as to the details.[2]

Personal opinions or ideas that may be good in particular cultures or geographical areas do have value—but they are not to be taken as universally revealed truth. Like barnacles, they attach themselves to the Old Ship of Zion, the church, and continue to hang on across the years until people believe them to be revealed truth. We need to let the Spirit of truth guide us into that truth which is essential to the saving of the soul and the sanctifying of our natures. In so doing, God always uses terminology that is understood universally. Terms like *birth, life, light, water,* and *death* are understood around the world. There must be understandable communication among us, even though we are different. This can only be done when we acknowledge that differences do exist among us. A few of these are racial, cultural, educational, economic, and emotional differences. We are also different in our receptivity of religious experience, our aesthetic appreciation of worship, our ability to perceive truth, and our ability to perform or produce. These differences accentuate our relational problems inside and outside the church. The good news, though, is that God has

---

[2]Deal, *Problems of the Spirit-Filled Life,* 37.

given to us particular graces that enable us to relate to other Christians in a healthy manner. Paul referred to these as longsuffering, gentleness, and goodness—more fruit of the Spirit.

Longsuffering

The Greek word for longsuffering is translated by our modern word *patience*. It reflects one's attitude toward people and events. In a day when people are anxious about many things, patience is very often misunderstood. Many people see patience as a weakness or an unwillingness to speak up for what could be rightly theirs. When people suffer long without losing their temper, others begin to question their courage. But patience is not passive; it is the long look of the Spirit-filled life. It is the quiet confidence that believes truth and love always win out in the final analysis. It is the belief that, when treated wrongly by other persons, forgiveness and acceptance should be exercised rather than vengeance.

This kind of longsuffering is referred to in Helmut Thielicke's sermon entitled "The Waiting Father," based on Luke 15. He accentuates the fact that the father could have broken off all relationship with the son. Rather than that, with a loving spirit, he patiently waited for the boy to find himself and return home. And when he did return home, there was no retaliation, no attempt to make the boy pay for his misdeeds. There was no probation period of holding him off at arm's length until he had proven himself.

God is patient beyond human understanding. Peter wrote, "The Lord… is patient with you, not wanting anyone to perish, but everyone to come to repentance" (2 Peter 3:9). It is this kind of patience that the Holy Spirit produces in our lives. It is a confident belief in people that enables us to have faith in them when others give up. It is a patience that holds onto hope when there is nothing but despair. And even when it makes us look like fools, we are "fools for Christ" (1 Cor 4:10). In such circumstances, we continue to strive, because that is the nature of the Holy Spirit.

Too often we have allowed people to be lost from the fellowship of the church, all because we were not longsuffering with one another in our interpersonal relationships. We become impatient and turn to others who may be more responsive, thus allowing others to feel rejected. There will be times when, because of our patience with another, we will feel that we have been taken advantage of. But at such times we can remember how patient Christ was with us until we responded positively to his love. We relate better to others when we discover the divine grace of patience.

Kindness

Most helpful in our human relationships is the fruit of kindness. While referred to as "gentleness" in the King James Version, the word *kindness* (from RSV and NIV) is more easily understood. Like the other fruit of the spirit in this triad, it deals with our contacts with other people.

We may have a kindly attitude, but unless it is tested in relating with other people it may be only an empty, meaningless word. Such testing may come at the most unexpected time—a time when someone disagrees with us or rubs us the wrong way, causing us to react bitterly. Maybe our proposal has been voted down by the board of directors. Maybe the children left a toy on the steps and someone is injured. It is in moments like these that we sometimes have a crop failure of the fruit of love, joy, peace, patience, and kindness.

Kindness is the ability to understand how another person feels. It means entering into another person's experience and conducting ourselves accordingly. It helps us understand other people, even when they have done wrong. Someone has called it "love's active consideration of others."

Isn't it true that all of the people with whom you've had a healthy relationship have expressed kindness? Theirs was not a condescending, paternalistic type of relationship. But in trying to understand you and help you, they demonstrated the fruit of kindness.

While the Holy Spirit has the power of a mighty rushing wind, the Spirit also has a quality that is as gentle as the breeze that one barely feels against the face. This is the quality of kindness.

Goodness

It is reported that Kagawa, the great Japanese Christian, said, "I read in a book that a man called Christ went about doing good. It is very disconcerting to me that I am so easily satisfied with just going about."[3] Many of our relational problems develop at this level. We are Christians, even Christians surrendered to the Holy Spirit, but we are seemingly content to just be involved in going about doing busywork. The goodness spoken of in Galatians is defined by Adam Clarke as "the perpetual desire and sincere study, not only to abstain from every appearance of evil, but to do good to the bodies and souls of man to the utmost of our ability."[4] There is a dual expectation in goodness: One is to abstain from all that would appear to be evil. The other is to do good

---

[3]Quoted in Barclay, *Daily Celebration*, 236.

[4]Clarke, *Clarke's Commentary*, 1166.

to those in need. James said, "Anyone, then, who knows the good he ought to do and doesn't do it, sins" (4:17). We have often been accused of overstressing the negative aspect of goodness while ignoring the dimension of social ministries to people all about us, people who are crying out for an expression of goodness on the part of the church. But the Holy Spirit never goes off on a tangent, overemphasizing one need above another. The Spirit-filled life is always one of balance, beauty, and symmetry.

Truly, Paul was inspired by the Holy Spirit when he wrote this great passage of Scripture in Galatians. With the wide variety of people in the world, God knew that only the Spirit could equip us to live in right relationship with one another.

FOR FURTHER STUDY:

1. What scriptural basis do you find for the implementation of holiness in the area of social ethics?

2. How responsible is the Spirit-filled person for maintaining proper relationships with other people?

3. In what way did the young church in Acts apply the Pentecostal experience to building Christian relationships among people of differing cultures?

4. How longsuffering should the sanctified person be? Is there a limit to how long one should suffer in working with other people?

5. Define *kindness* as referred to in Paul's listing of the fruit of the Spirit. Give examples of this type of relationship.

6. Could one be filled with the Spirit and fail to measure up to the standards set forth in the Sermon on the Mount? Read the account given in Matthew 5, 6, and 7; then note the different relationships required of God's people.

7. With the strong emphasis on evangelism, why do many holiness people find it difficult to relate to individuals who may differ with them theologically? Can we not be patient, kind, and good—even with those who may differ with us theologically?

8. Make a list of the ways the fruit of the Spirit may be helpful in our relationships within the family, between husband and wife, or parents and children.

The *fruit of the Spirit* is…
faithfulness,
gentleness,
and *self-control*.…

—GALATIANS 5:22–23

HIS SPIRIT
AND
MY DISCIPLINE

Our people too often get an emotional experience of "sanctification"
which is totally unrelated in their thinking to any form of rugged self-
denial. They are not apt to obtain genuine holiness of heart unless they
see clearly in advance that holiness both implies and demands discipline,
in all its forms and facets and at all levels of daily living.

Richard Shelley Taylor
The Disciplined Life, 13
(emphasis added)

9

His Spirit and My Discipline

PERSONAL DISCIPLINE is demanded in the discipleship of the Spirit. While we have looked at what God does for us through the infilling of the Holy Spirit, we would be less than honest if we did not stress the need for our implementation of grace through discipline. "In a general sense, self-discipline is the ability to regulate conduct by principle and judgment, rather than impulse, desire, high pressure, or social custom. It is basically the ability to subordinate."[1] While we believe that the Holy Spirit cleanses the heart of the believer, there still remains the biblical requirement for self-denial and for cross bearing.

Too many Christians have heard glowing sermons on the miraculous power of the Spirit to transform our natures and they have assumed that this experience will overcome all their human weaknesses. Such people have interpreted this teaching to mean that certain habits will be overcome if they can truly be filled with the Spirit. If this myth could be destroyed, our theology of the Holy Spirit would be much more easily understood and much healthier in the life of the church.

While his indwelling presence does make power available to overcome habits, it is necessary for the believer to bring the self into compliance with this total commitment. Howard Thurman, in his book *Disciplines of the Spirit*, writes, "The meaning of commitment as a discipline of the Spirit must take into account that mind and spirit cannot be separated from the body in any absolute sense."[2]

---

[1] Taylor, *Disciplined Life*, 26.
[2] Thurman, *Disciplines of the Spirit*, 17.

We must begin a practical implementation of those disciplines that will help us to become mature persons in Christ. Even with the power of the Holy Spirit, we must exercise persistent determination to develop consistent discipline.

What are some of the manifestations of undisciplined living? The items below could be listed in response. One should be extremely careful, though, in always relating these to the lack of discipline, since they may also be caused by other things. However, they are often found where there is a lack of personal discipline:

> Restlessness and instability
> Running from difficult assignments
> Avoiding incompatible people
> Moral looseness
> Shallowness in stewardship of life
> Spiritual laziness

We will not always be anxious to be disciplined just because we are surrendered to the Spirit. There remains in all of us what Dr. Hugh Missildine has called "your inner child of the past." He deals with the concept that there is a "child" within all of us that seeks its own way, acting out those attitudes developed during the formative years.[3] Some of these attitudes show themselves in church business meetings, in person-to-person relationships, and even within the family. Does that mean that we are unsanctified? That we have lost the Holy Spirit from our lives? Certainly not! But when such demonstrations are recognized for the childish attitudes that they express, we can bring our lives under a discipline that produces maturity in the faith. In no way does this support the psychological strategy of suppression. It is only the honest admission that there remains in all of us that human nature which wants its way rather than God's way. For that reason, Paul said, "I put childish things behind me" (1 Cor 13:11). He pursued the more "excellent way" of loving God with all his soul and ministering to his neighbor rather than pampering his inner child.

Such discipline is needed in many areas of our lives after we have been filled with the Holy Spirit. Paul refers to both body and mind in Romans 12. He speaks of presenting our bodies and of renewing our minds, neither of which takes place automatically upon being sanctified.

While Paul specifically mentions these two areas—body and mind—every dimension of our lives must be brought under the discipline of the

---

[3]Missildine, *Your Inner Child of the Past.*

Spirit. Discipline will affect our devotional life, our responsiveness to the Spirit's leadership, and our obedience to God's Word. To be filled with the Spirit means that he dwells within us and, as he directs, we bring our bodies into compliance with God's will to us through him. Kenneth Geiger, in a paper on "Sanctification and Growth," comments, "This is the process wherein the Holy Spirit through *willingly accepted disciplines*, enables the sanctified Christian to overcome objectionable temperaments and other personality traits which so often distort the image of Christ projected to the world."[4] I have underscored the words *willingly accepted disciplines*, for what we are speaking about is not something that God makes me do. Rather, out of the more excellent way of love, I have become a love-slave, seeking only the highest and holiest: God's plan for my life.

It is because of the need for self-discipline in the Spirit-filled life that the last cluster of Spirit fruit deals with the inner self—faithfulness, humility, and self-control. All of these are self-imposed because they reflect the nature of the Holy Spirit, who dwells within us.

Faith

Faith reveals again the nature of the Spirit of God—one who loved us and sought us persistently until we surrendered to his will for our lives. He was *faithful* to us. It is this quality to which the fruit of the Spirit refers. Through the power of the Holy Spirit, we bring ourselves to a place of loyal devotion, fidelity, and lasting commitment to Christ. It is the power to stand and "after [we] have done everything, to stand" (Eph 6:13). It is the kind of faith demonstrated by Job, who said in the midst of life's difficulties, "Though he slay me, yet will I hope in him [remain faithful, believe]" (Job 13:15). It is the willingness, if need be, to "contend for the faith that was once for all entrusted to the saints" (Jude v. 3).

Such faithfulness is not born of easy living or casualness. It is the result of the disciplined life that seeks first the kingdom of God (cf. Matt 6:33), regardless of the cost or what others may do. Within the word *faith*, there is a resoluteness of purpose, a willingness to endure, even in the midst of the most severe storm or struggle.

Jesus said, "He who stands firm to the end will be saved" (Matt 10:22). The Master had just spoken of how his followers would be hated for his name's sake. They would face family conflict, and they would be severely persecuted. But in the midst of all this, they were to remain faithful. Though some may give up, there is a dimension of faithfulness to God

---

[4]In Boyd and Harris, *Projecting Our Heritage*, 135, italics added.

and others that keeps us true. It is not easy—but who said discipline was easy? It is the high cost of holiness. God wants believers to be faithful even unto death.

Meekness

Here is a discipline that is often needed but not recognized by those who may need it the most—*humility!* We are not born humble. There is something within us that seeks attention. It develops into selfish pride and arrogance.

Now, not all pride is bad. It can be very helpful when it is kept in proper balance. This kind of positive pride is produced in the believer through the discipline of the Spirit.

Too often we have been guilty of a pretentious type of humility—appearing quiet, subdued, and reserved, while within us there burns the desire to be recognized. When we are sanctified, the Spirit does not remove our pride. But he will cleanse our natures, granting us power to develop a humble attitude about ourselves and our abilities. It brings to our life a strength and sensitivity that is both tough and tender—the ability to not need to demonstrate power to possess it. When Jesus said that the meek shall inherit the earth (Matt 5:5), he indicated a strength born of the Spirit within.

Remember the words of Philippians 2:5–8:

> Your attitude should be the same as that of Christ Jesus: Who, being in very nature God, did not consider equality with God something to be grasped, but made himself nothing, taking the very nature of a servant, being made in human likeness. And being found in appearance as a man, he humbled himself and became obedient to death—even death on a cross!

Self-control

While some have chosen to refer to this Spirit-fruit as "Spirit-control"—implying that the Spirit is in control of one's life—I would prefer the term as used in the Revised Standard Version: *self-control.* Certainly the Spirit-filled life is one wherein we yield to his complete will. However, it is wrong to imply that when the Spirit is in control, we can no longer exercise our power of free moral choice. Therefore, we speak of *self-control* through the power of the Spirit.

Perhaps none of the fruit mentioned in Galatians 5 is more vital to our modeling of holiness than self-control. Only through this grace can we maintain spiritual stability, intellectual integrity, moral purity, and social sensitivity. God's Spirit enables us to practice discipline in our personal lives.

As we conclude these three chapters on the fruit of the Spirit, let us reflect on the areas considered. On the God-ward side, we have love, joy, and peace produced by his Spirit in our personalities. In our relationships on the human side, there is the fruit of longsuffering, kindness, and goodness expressed toward those with whom we live. Inwardly, the fruit produced is faithfulness, meekness, and self-control—all demanding discipline as we continue to grow by his grace.

FOR FURTHER STUDY:

1. Consider and evaluate the human discipline implied in the following verses: Romans 12:1–2 and 2 Corinthians 7:1.

2. Examine the difference between the *cleansing* of the appetites and the *discipline* of the appetites. Are they the same, or is there an interrelatedness?

3. Study 1 Corinthians 9:27 as it relates to the concept of discipline in the Spirit. Are we accountable for controlling this body in which the Spirit dwells?

4. To be zealous of good works is commendable, but sometimes our zeal outweighs our wisdom. How can the Spirit-filled person discipline this zeal without losing the enthusiasm needed for the things of God?

Now there are diversities of *gifts*,
but the same Spirit.

—1 CORINTHIANS 12:4, KJV

CHARISMATA:
THE GIFTS
OF THE SPIRIT

Every Believer has some gift. This does not mean that everyone is exercising the gift or gifts with which the Spirit has endowed him/her. Nor does everyone necessarily know what his/her gift is. But it is clear that every Christian has been given at least one gift which is to be exercised in the upbuilding of the Church.

J. Oswald Sanders
The Holy Spirit and His Gifts, 110
(emphasis added)

10

Charismata:
The Gifts of the Spirit

SPIRITUAL GIFTS are essential to fulfilling the mission of the church. Jesus instructed the disciples to "wait" for the promise of the Father (Acts 1:4) before they began to witness. Paul writes concerning the spiritual gifts (1 Cor 12:1) needed for the church's ministry. If the young church was to fulfill its mission in the world, spiritual gifts must be recognized and properly exercised.

Although the Holy Spirit's gifts had been received, controversy developed in the Corinthian congregation as to how these gifts should be used. The importance of the subject is not to be overlooked. In three of his epistles—Romans, 1 Corinthians, and Ephesians—Paul gives attention to this truth. When one views the confusion and controversy about gifts in the church today, it is easy to see why Paul wanted to be very clear in teaching about this aspect of the Holy Spirit. While the fruit of the Spirit is a part of every sanctified believer's life, reproducing in us the nature of Christlikeness, the gifts of the Spirit are not demonstrated in every life, nor are they fully understood.

Even our terminology is difficult to understand. *Charismata*—what does it mean? Basically, this Greek word is related to grace, for *charis* means "grace." It implies something we do not merit or earn; only through the goodness of God is it received. Paul uses this expression in Romans 6:23 when speaking of our salvation. He uses the term most often, though, in referring to the *charismata* of the Holy Spirit. These gifts given in grace are entirely undeserved, and all that is accomplished through their use is due to the Spirit's power.

Bible scholars have used different formulas to delineate the various gifts mentioned in the New Testament. At least two of these will be outlined to give assistance in our study and to serve as an example of how others have approached the subject. The gifts entrusted to us are determined by the type of ministry to which God has called us. Often, the spiritual gifts may be an amplification of our natural gifts. Such gifts, however, exceed the purely human ability as the Holy Spirit works in and through the yielded life. At other times, God may entrust to us a gift that is totally unrelated to our human abilities. Again, the gifts are not determined by our natural potential, but by the ministry to which the Lord has called us. If called to speak, the Holy Spirit enables us to communicate. If our calling is to serve in the most difficult of circumstances, God's Holy Spirit equips us to minister. If the Master has called us to bring healing to the sick, he will not fail to provide the power for the miraculous. Therefore, some divide the gifts into these three general areas: *speaking* gifts; *serving* gifts; *signifying* gifts. Others prefer to use terms relating to the type of ministry carried out, such as the ministry of *helping*, the ministry of *directing others*, the ministry of the *Word*, and the ministry of the *spectacular*. Each pattern merely becomes a formula to help the student recognize the divine enduement for service and the responsibility to be stewards of these gifts.

Qualifications

God commissioned the church. Through the Holy Spirit, he has equipped the church for ministry. Speaking to the disciples, Jesus said, "Anyone who has faith in me will do what I have been doing. He will do *even greater things* than these, because I am going to the Father" (John 14:12). Christ, the Head of the church, assures us of the power available through the Spirit. But he stipulates that the gifted person must have believing faith in order to receive this power. Paul affirms this in Romans 13:3 and in 1 Corinthians 13:13. He refers not only to the believing faith that claims the salvation of Christ but also to the faith that walks in obedience to his Word. Faith is required of those who *bear* the fruit of the Spirit; it is also required of those who would *exercise* the gifts of the Spirit.

Faith is born of love—loving God, his Word, and his church. Implied in this relationship is unwavering obedience in all that God has called us to do (Eph 4:1). We not only believe his truth, but we also believe that he calls us to a life of holiness. Such faith develops a consistent, stable Christian life.

There is a tendency to misuse and abuse spiritual gifts when there is not a satisfying spiritual experience in the life of the individual. When our faith is uncertain, our humanness is tempted to seek the spectacular gifts rather than finding contentment in the giver. Too often this becomes an ego trip for the seeker, defeating the very purpose for which the gifts are primarily given—service. The qualification for receiving gifts is faith in the Lord Jesus Christ.

But spirituality in itself does not qualify us for a particular gift. Paul states that God gives "as he determines" (1 Cor 12:11), and although you have a vital spiritual experience, God, may not see fit to give you a particular gift. Gifts are not given because of spirituality or age or status. They are given as God sees the need. In infinite wisdom, he provides a person with the gift to meet the need at that time.

The gifts of the Spirit are also misused when we are not producing the fruit of the Spirit. Failing to have produced humility and self-control, we abuse the gift entrusted to us. Our receiving of a gift of the Spirit does not guarantee that we will use it properly. The glory of grace gifts is that God does not hesitate to entrust them to us when we are willing to surrender to him. Human nature would become extremely cautious, wanting some assurance that everything would be right. But God still gives to us the Holy Spirit and risks bestowing upon us gifts for service in the body of Christ.

Consideration of Gifts

The task of the church as outlined in Matthew 28:19–20 would appear to be beyond our human capabilities. Yet God has assured us that "everything is possible for him who believes" (Mark 9:23). Believing faith opens to us the resources of God for fulfilling his Great Commission. Through the Spirit, we have been given new life in Christ. Then, as the life-giving Spirit rules within us, we are placed in the Body as it pleases him (1 Cor 12:18). For that reason, there are varieties of gifts (1 Cor 12:6), with at least eighteen bestowments being mentioned in the Pauline texts. I believe that these are not exhaustive, but only indicative of the power available through the Spirit to provide adequate ministry for any need that may arise within the body of Christ, the church.

It is obviously true that the resources of the Spirit are inexhaustible. While some gifts may render a greater service than others, they should never elevate one believer above another (1 Cor 12:14–25). Nor should we seek to restrict the exercising of particular gifts because of the individual's status in life. God is sovereign and he has chosen to distribute the gifts in the way most profitable for his kingdom.

Listings of the gifts are given in different ways, but they may be found in the Pauline writings as follows:

Romans 12:6–8	1 Corinthians 12:8–11	Ephesians 4:11
Prophecy	Wisdom	Apostles
Ministry	Knowledge	Prophets
Teaching	Faith	Evangelists
Encouraging	Healing	Pastors
Giving	Miracles	Teachers
Ruling	Prophecy	
Mercy	Discernment	
	Tongues	

In each instance, we find that love is the controlling factor for the exercising of the gifts of the Spirit (cf. Rom 12:9; 1 Cor 12:31; Eph 4:15).

Administration

Two verses serve as the basis for this guideline regarding the administration of the gifts of the Spirit. With a variety of persons and a diversity of gifts, competition may develop. The account of the Corinthian church would indicate that this happened in their midst. Sin had created not only problems of morality but also an attitude of competition for attention and leadership through the exaltation of particular gifts. Such problems are experienced in the church today. Because of this, God has given us instructions regarding who should administer the gifts to the members of the church and who should determine where they are to serve. God never entrusted the bestowal of gifts into the hands of a committee or board. He knew well the tendency of such groups to depend upon human intellect rather than divine inspiration and revelation. While boards, committees, and congregations may recognize through ordination those persons who possess the gifts of the Spirit, they do not dispense the gifts. God alone knows the needs and the places where each member of the Body can serve most adequately. Therefore, he divides "to each one, just as he determines" (1 Cor 12:11). In administering the gifts, he gives them to individuals, not to congregations. While it sometimes appears that gifts are given only to the large, successful congregations, Scripture states that God's will, not the size or influence of a church, determines the gifts bestowed. Therefore, the congregation that is ministering to human need, involving all of its people in service, can expect gifts that are in keeping with its ministry of witness and the Word. God may even grant to some individuals more than one gift. Here again, it is determined not by the person but by what God desires to do through that person.

Not all of the gifts were for a professional type of ministry. We are guilty of placing undue emphasis on such distinctions as clergy and laity, which were not a part of the New Testament church. Every task is important and all persons should exercise their gift within the life of the church. "One of the greatest losses which the passing of the centuries has brought to the church is the loss of the craftsman. The craftsman would be rediscovered in the church, his gifts would be rededicated to the church, if we would stop erecting a false spiritual aristocracy, if we would remember that the word *ministry* simply means *service,* and if we remember that any gift which a man has is a gift of the Spirit, and can be laid on the altar of the service of God."[1] These words of William Barclay challenge the church to allow the exercising of the gifts God has granted to his children.

In administering the gifts, God places the "members every one of them in the body, as it hath pleased him" (1 Cor 12:18, KJV). We neither choose the gift we desire nor select our place of service. The sovereign God, who knows all things, places each person individually where it pleases him. If left to human choice, it would be easy to allow our emotional and physical feelings to determine our decisions. But when surrendered to the Holy Spirit, controlled by God's will and purpose, we are placed where we can make the greatest contribution to the life of the church. Always preeminent in the Christian life is the desire to serve where God places us. This does not, as some appear to believe, mean that he always places us in a difficult place of adversity. One is not more spiritual because of serving in difficult places. God places us where we can be of the greatest service, and in such circumstances, he gives grace to adjust to those things that may be disagreeable.

Variations

Every Christian is of significant value and has a contribution to make to the church. While some congregations seek to control both persons and

---

[1]Barclay, *Promise of the Spirit,* 84.

programs, the successful congregation is one wherein all persons are encouraged to discover and develop their gifts. Such openness in the church requires a quality of spiritual maturity similar to that exemplified at Pentecost. It requires a pastor who is secure enough not to be threatened by members of the congregation who have greater ability. It also requires a congregation that is trusting and accepting of new members whom God has placed in the Body, allowing them to exercise their gifts. Many a potentially powerful congregation has been thwarted in attempts to grow, simply because they have not been willing to accept the variety of people and gifts God has placed in the church.

While open to the more traditional gifts of preaching, teaching, and healing, we are not as open to the other gifts mentioned in Scripture. Within any congregation, it is possible that there may be a wide variation of gifts. We are in error to expect a particular gift in our congregation simply because we have witnessed it in another group of believers. The bestowment of gifts, as already indicated, is due to the specific need of the particular group.

The wide range of cultures, religious backgrounds, and economic influences surrounding people and congregations cannot be ignored. Each congregation demands a particular type of gift to meet its specific needs. Because of this, there are variations in the gifts bestowed by God upon his people. While no one gift is common to all, it is also true that no one person possesses all the gifts. Romans 12:6 ("We have different gifts, according to the grace given us") and 1 Corinthians 12:4 ("There are different kinds of gifts") would reveal that, while given by the same Spirit, there are varieties of people used and varieties of gifts bestowed.

Clarification

In the midst of an inspiring and enthusiastic service of worship, it is easy to allow our emotions to control our conduct. Although God had fulfilled his promise in giving the Spirit and bestowing gifts upon the Corinthian church, not everyone in the church exercised these gifts in a manner acceptable and edifying to the Body. After speaking about the diversity of gifts, Paul admonishes the Corinthians regarding the use of the gifts. He gives a priority listing of the *charismata* in 1 Corinthians, hoping to correct an error that had developed due to an overemphasis on the gift of tongues.

In their services of worship, their enthusiasm bordered on the ecstatic. While not wanting to quench their spirit of enthusiasm, Paul did want to give direction regarding the value of gifts. Therefore, he prioritized them as follows: apostles, prophets, teachers, miracles, healings, helps, governments, tongues (1 Cor 12:28). Clarence Tucker Craig writes: "The order in which the ministries are named is deliberate: the apostles have received the highest gift and the speakers in tongues the lowest."[2]

Paul is manifesting the fruit of the Spirit in his own attitude. Though firm in his conviction, his letter is one of love and Christian courtesy. Too often in attempting to clarify misunderstandings about the *charismata,* we speak harshly and judgmentally, preaching *at* people rather than speaking *to* and *with* them. Love, of which he writes so eloquently, is lived out so appropriately in these three chapters, twelve through fourteen. They serve as a Pauline guide to the proper exercising of *charismata.*

Paul's spirit of understanding was no doubt prompted by his knowledge that God had given a gift of languages. The Corinthian experience was some twenty years following Pentecost, and in that time, Paul had become thoroughly informed regarding the outpouring of the Spirit at Jerusalem (Acts 2), Caesarea (ch. 10), and Ephesus (ch. 19). In none of his writings has he felt inclined to speak on this issue until the exercising of the gift reflected that which was not genuine. So long as the gifts are used rightly in the Spirit of love, building up the Body, relating properly to all other gifts in the Body, there is no reason to take corrective measures. However, when error has crept in, one must speak the truth in love, leaving no doubt as to the intent of God's Word. Wherever there is a real gift of the Spirit, there are those who would seek to reproduce it in the flesh. And while there may have been a real gift of languages used for the glory of God in Corinth, it created a desire that attracted more attention for this gift than the less demonstrative gifts. Nowhere are we admonished to seek specific gifts, only to seek the giver, the Holy Spirit. Because of the undue importance placed upon this particular gift at Corinth, persons were seeking it, and some were even reproducing it in their own human ability. Charles Carter writes:

> The tongues problem at Corinth obviously consisted in a confusion and consequent counterfeiting of the genuine, miraculously, bestowed gift of *bona fide* languages, such as was experienced at the Jerusalem Pentecost, at Caesarea, and at Ephesus. Some Corinthian Christians apparently introduced in the church elements of the unintelligible, ecstatic utterances used by the worshipers of

[2]Craig, *Interpreter's Bible,* Vol. X, 163.

Aphrodite and Cybele at Corinth, and elsewhere in the ancient world. Many in the church at Corinth had doubtless worshiped at the shrines of the lustful goddess Aphrodite Pandemos and Cybele before their conversion to Christianity. In this worship, trances and ecstatic experiences, accompanied by unintelligible and meaningless utterances, were common."[4]

It is out of the context of this Corinthian confusion that Paul writes, giving spiritual principles that apply not only to this particular gift but to all charismata. Dr. Boyce Blackwelder speaks to this in his commentary on 1 Corinthians 14:5:

> Paul is dealing with young converts, many of whom were former pagans. Some faults of their pre-Christian experience were reappearing or, more probably, had not yet been overcome. The Corinthians needed to understand the nature of Spiritual gifts, and to escape the peril of false expressions. Pagan worship was characterized by frenzied, ecstatic utterances over which reason had no control. Paul does not approve unreasoning emotionalism. His purpose is to lead the Christian believer completely away from the old cultic behavior patterns. To this end he writes in a diplomatic manner and takes a positive approach, emphasizing the qualities and procedures which are paramount in the new life.[5]

It is because such confusion exists in the church today that clarification is called for regarding the *charismata*. The problem is not that there are no real gifts bestowed by the Holy Spirit, but that we are prone to misuse or abuse the gifts. Wherever there is real divine healing, one also finds charlatans who exploit the gift for financial gain. Wherever there is a true gift of preaching, there are those who through eloquence and oratory manipulate the people who would hear the message. And wherever there is a true gift of language bestowed as God wills, there are those who defeat the purpose by elevating it to a place of spiritual superiority. This Paul openly denounces.

Much of today's controversy regarding the *charismata* and the ministry of the Holy Spirit is due to particular factions of the community of

---

[3]Carter, *Person and Ministry of the Holy Spirit*, n.p.

[4]Blackwelder, *Letters from Paul*, 64.

faith who have made the gift of tongues the evidence of being filled with the Spirit. It is too easy for persons to test truth by experience rather than evaluating the experience by divinely inspired and revealed truth. To clarify the gifts of the Spirit within the church, we must always return to our source, the inspired Scriptures. It is here that the Holy Spirit is able to lead us into "all truth," if we seek his leadership in humility.

From the Corinthian account, where the problem arose, we have reason to believe that there is a true gift of communication among the *charismata*. To deny the existence of the gift is to be less than honest with Scripture. Many have been as much in error at this point as those who have made this singular gift the evidence of the Spirit-filled life.

Having acknowledged the bestowal of such a gift, what are the principles governing the use of gifts in the church?

First, *the giver is more important than the gift*. One should never seek for power, signs, or evidence, but rather seek the Spirit, who bestows gifts "as he determines."

Second, *gifts are always governed by the fruit of the Spirit, basic of which is love*. As previously stated, in all of Paul's writings about the *charismata*, the qualifying factor is an attitude of divine love.

Finally, *the gifts are always given for the building up of the body of Christ*. No gift is for selfish exaltation. Serious questions should be asked if one claims a gift of the Spirit and is haughty or proud. At such times, one would be wise to exercise the instruction of 1 John 4:1: "Dear friends, do not believe every spirit, but test the spirits to see whether they are from God, because many false prophets have gone out into the world."

Unity

Essential in our study of the *charismata* is the purpose for which they are given. True, they are to edify the Body; but this can be accomplished only when there is unity within the church.

Too often the one doctrine that has divided the church has been that of the Holy Spirit. We would do well to heed the counsel of Peter Gillquist in the title of his book *Let's Quit Fighting about the Holy Spirit*. God's intent is that the church should be one. It was this for which Jesus prayed. It is this which came to pass at the Jerusalem Pentecost. However, in our attempt to be theologically circumspect, we sometimes cut ourselves off from other Christians whom God would have us recognize as his children. There is one Body (1 Cor 12:12; Rom 12:4–5; Eph 4:4), which is the result of being born of the Spirit. God has seen fit to place each of us in the

Body where we can function most effectively. To accomplish that purpose, he has given to us the *charismata* for the obvious reasons of perfecting the saints, the work of ministry, and the edification of the Body (Eph 4:12). And as members of the same Body, we carry a mutual concern for the other members—regardless of where they may serve—remembering that no one is unimportant and no task is insignificant.

FOR FURTHER STUDY:

1. Which has greater influence for Christ, a spectacular gift or a consistent character of holiness?

2. What scriptures indicate that not all gifts are of God? Share some of these verses and discuss them.

3. How many gifts are spoken of in the New Testament? Are these the only gifts? Give a reason for your answer.

4. What is your personal response to the emphasis on *charismata* today? Can you give a scriptural basis for your personal conviction regarding this teaching?

5. Is there a danger of becoming obsessed with a concern for gifts of the Spirit? What possible dangers might develop?

6. The Holy Spirit is clearly portrayed as a unifying factor in New Testament faith. Why is it, then, that we find division in the Christian faith over the Holy Spirit?

7. How would you recommend that we maintain a proper balance between the fruit of the Spirit and the gifts bestowed?

The *Helper,* the *Holy Spirit,*
whom the Father will send in My name,
He will teach you all things, and bring to remembrance
all that I said to you.

—JOHN 14:26, NASB

OUR HELPER
TO
HEALING

We need to confront the simplistic heresies that distort this biblical teaching: such as the idea that lack of healing is caused by inadequate faith or unconfessed sin hidden in the sufferer's life; or if our prayers don't work, that there is something wrong with the one who prayed. Our task is to help bring people to the Great Physician.

Lloyd John Ogilvie
Why Not?, 11

11

Our Helper for Healing

CATHERINE MARSHALL, wife of Peter Marshall, chaplain of the United States Senate from 1947 to 1949, gives us an account of her personal experience with the Holy Spirit in her book *The Helper*. In her experience with the Holy Spirit in 1943, he enabled her to appropriate God's healing power for a debilitating lung disease. Rather than experiencing immediate, miraculous healing, she experienced the Holy Spirit as Comforter, Counselor, and Helper. The Holy Spirit became her Helper to healing as she struggled with what appeared to be unanswered prayer, teaching her to allow God to bring wholeness to her life.

Sadly, there are many who believe that if the sick are not healed immediately, then their faith is too weak or there must be some sin in their life. Once while I was pastoring, our worship leader came to me with an urgent prayer request for a relative experiencing severe depression. After we had prayed together, he shared with me a testimony of the relative's dedicated Christian life. Then he added, "If she had really been sanctified, this would never have happened." How tragic! Yet, while not stating it so bluntly, there are many holiness people who live under the same delusion.

The Holy Spirit transforms the heart, not the body. As stated in this book, sanctification cleanses the heart, but it does not remove anything that is essentially human. Contrary to what some appear to believe, holiness people are still human. Holiness is not health insurance, nor is sanctification a panacea for sickness and suffering. Those models of the deeper Spirit-filled life have often passed through severe suffering due to physical or emotional infirmities. As long as we are in the body, we will be subject to the weaknesses of the flesh.

It is here that the Holy Spirit becomes our Helper for healing. The Holy Spirit is not the Healer, but as our Helper, he enables us to remember (call to mind) and to experience (claim the promises of) the healing available through Christ. Jesus said, "The Helper, the Holy Spirit, whom the Father will send in My name, He will teach you all things, and bring to your remembrance all that I said unto you" (John 14:26, NASB).

It is true that Scripture teaches us that our bodies are the temple of the Holy Spirit (1 Cor 6:19). But Scripture also emphasizes, in 2 Corinthians 4:7, that this treasure is in earthen vessels; the words used in this passage indicate a very fragile clay pot, one that can be easily broken. This brokenness becomes more apparent in our lives each day. Broken bodies, tormented minds, sickness, and disease leave no question about our need for healing. Like writers of old, we ask, "Is there no balm in Gilead? Is there no physician there?" (Jer 8:22). Even with the enlightenment of our Helper, we forget that not everyone was healed when Jesus was physically here on earth. We also fail to grasp that healing is not permanent; even those resurrected by the Healer (John 11:43–44) eventually died (Heb 9:27).

Divine healing is beyond our human comprehension; it is supernatural and miraculous. However, divine healing is real, and God has given us the Holy Spirit to help us properly understand the Scriptures and appropriate God's promises for our physical and spiritual needs. He helps us discern between truth and error in matters of healing and wholeness. Only the Helper, the Holy Spirit, can enable us to rightly know the Healer, for Jesus said, "He will testify about me" (John 15:26).

Helping Our Unbelief

Faith is the indispensable ingredient in salvation, the healing of the soul (Eph 2:8–9). It is also the basic requirement for physical healing. When the woman who had been ill for twelve years reached out in the crowd and touched the fringe of Jesus' cloak, she was made whole immediately. In the conversation that followed, Jesus said, "Your faith has healed you" (Luke 8:48). All healing—spiritual, physical, emotional, and relational—begins with faith. Not all healing is immediate, however, and in the midst of our pain and distress, we often find it difficult to believe. With the father in Mark 9, we confess, "I do believe; help me overcome my unbelief" (v. 24). We too believe in Christ, his Word, and the church, but sometimes it is difficult to claim that which is ours as a child of God. The Helper then comes to stir up our minds, making us aware once again of Christ's promises to us and of his divine Presence with us. When the words of the physician, the counselor, or the psychiatrist are inadequate to meet our deep needs, we cry out, "God, help our weak faith!"

Preaching divine healing is much easier before one experiences a critical illness or faces family sickness. As a young pastor, I believed deeply in divine healing and preached it. However, my belief was tested when severe sickness came into my family's home. Confronted by doctors unable to correct the problem, we earnestly sought the Lord. We tried to believe! In obedience to God's Word, we called in the elders of the church, anointed the afflicted one with oil, and prayed the prayer of faith, but no miracle happened. Repeatedly, we were driven to our knees in prayer as we sought the Lord in tears, wanting so much to believe. It was then that the Helper came, assuring us of God's unfailing love.

Note that the Holy Spirit did not do the healing, nor did he guarantee that healing would come. But the Holy Spirit did help us remember that God, through Christ, was the Healer, even when our hearts were breaking.

In that dark night of the soul, the Helper brought to mind instances of healing from God's Word that had required great faith. Naaman's leprosy was cleansed when he obediently dipped himself in the muddy Jordan seven times (2 Kings 5:11–17). The man at the pool of Bethesda, crippled for thirty-eight years, wanted someone to help him into the healing waters, but Jesus made him well (John 5:1-9). The Helper reminded me of how dependent we are on God's power for healing.

But what about consulting a physician? Would that hinder the healing for which I prayed? The Helper brought to my mind the woman who had spent all her money on physicians (Luke 8:43). That she had visited doctors did not matter to the Great Physician—he did not condemn her; rather he made her well.

When the Holy Spirit brought all this to mind, I realized that sometimes God heals miraculously, instantaneously, and that at other times he heals through the wise counsel and ministry of physicians, surgeons, counselors, pastors, and caring nurses. Faith for healing requires that when we cannot see clearly, we allow the Helper to guide us through the darkness. After six years, the healing came; it came through prayer, medical science, the skill of surgeons, and the ministry of a loving church. The greatest healing was not physical; rather it was the healing of our faith as the Helper enabled us to believe that all things are possible in Christ (Mark 9:23). Christ is the Healer; he mends broken hearts, opens eyes to understanding, and helps us hear the wind of the Spirit as we believe.

Help from a Healing Community

God planned for the church to be a healing community—not a hospital, but a body of believers made whole by the wounded Healer. The help we need in times of suffering cannot come from one who knows nothing of human pain, anxiety, and fear. Dietrich Bonhoeffer, writing out of the sickness, suffering, and loneliness of a wartime prison, said that "only a suffering God can help us."[1] Our belief in the incarnation reveals that God took upon himself the form of a servant made in the likeness of man and became obedient unto death, even death on the cross (Phil 2:5–11). The Helper then enables us to understand that our high priest can "sympathize with our weaknesses" because he became like us in every way (Heb 4:15). Each tear that falls, each pain we feel, all of the anger and hatred we experience—Christ experienced it all for our healing. Isaiah 53 portrays this suffering God, who, through Christ, became the Great Physician, the Healer.

Seeing people as sheep without a shepherd, Jesus was moved with compassion and healed them (John 9:35–36). He requires this same compassion of the church. History reveals that the church has made a great contribution to the world through a compassionate, loving, healing ministry. The church triumphant must first become a community of servant healers.

How blessed are Christians who worship in churches that believe and practice divine healing. Such congregations have an atmosphere of expectancy: They believe that God can and will heal as we call upon him in prayer.

Holiness Holds Us Together

John Wesley referred to holiness as perfect love—a love that will not let us go or give up on us, but a love that continues to reach out and hold us even when we are hurting. Love, acceptance, understanding, and forgiveness create an atmosphere in which healing takes place. It is an atmosphere that allows for transparency and openness without fear of rejection, retaliation, or isolation, and it is an environment that permits questioning, doubting, and seeking for answers in the fulfillment of "seek and you will find; knock and the door will be opened to you" (Matt 7:7). In this environment, we come to understand Scripture's teaching on healing; we feel free to question and to let the Helper direct our quest.

---

[1]As quoted in a sermon by Peter W. Marty, Sunday, February 27, 2005, "Grace Matters: Shaking Your Fist at God, Suffering Part 1" at the Evangelical Lutheran Church of America, 8765 W. Higgins Road, Chicago, IL 60631.

In contrast, a critical, caustic, condemning congregation, often led by negative, legalistic preaching and teaching, causes brokenness and hinders healing. We grieve the Holy Spirit (Eph 4:30) when we permit such opinions and attitudes to prevail. The Helper reminds us that "God didn't go to all the trouble of sending his Son merely to point an accusing finger, telling the world how bad it was. He came to help, to put the world right again" (John 3:17, MSG). Only when the church exhibits the very nature of Christ—bearing one another's burdens, weeping with those who weep, turning the other cheek, and going the second mile—do we become the healing community that God intended.

Healing Is God's Gift

The Holy Spirit, our Helper, equips the church to fulfill her ministry. Among the gifts entrusted to the church by the Spirit is the gift of healing (1 Cor 12:9). Correctly stated, this phrase is plural in Greek, "gifts of healings," indicating that healing is the ministry of the whole Body. Every gift of the Spirit is given for the "common good" (12:7), but it is only when all members of the Body are exercising their gifts and fulfilling their proper roles that a healthy church develops. The ministry of healing is not for an elected body or appointed leaders, not just for the highly visible persons in the household of faith. Rather, it is the ministry of the total congregation.

It is true, however, that some within the Body receive a unique gift of healing because God has chosen to use them in this type of ministry. Their consistent example of Christian holiness, humility, and obedience to the Holy Spirit generates faith for healing.

Our Helper, the Holy Spirit, gives us a sense of discernment. At no time in our lives are we more vulnerable than when faced with the news of an incurable or terminal illness. In seeking help, we tend to grasp for straws, desiring to believe what we know is not true. Self-proclaimed faith healers often abuse the truth of healing by exploiting the sick and afflicted, manipulating them for monetary gain; they assure the innocent and unsuspecting that God will heal their bodies and meet all their needs. But healing is a gift, a gift to be exercised within the church for the glory of God. It is not a gift to be exploited at mass healing meetings and on high-pressure television programs in order to boost the egos and ratings of independent self-styled healers. Jesus was moved with compassion for the sick; he was not motivated by the profit margin of his program.

Help Is Available

Inspired by the Holy Spirit, James explains how to seek healing (5:14–15). The simplicity of the steps outlined causes us to overlook the truth that God is accessible and that healing is available. James's words are too often used as a last resort when we have tried everything else. When all else fails, read the directions: "Is any one of you sick…call…" Human need, sickness, will confront all of us at some point in our lifetime. When it does, we are to "call" because God is waiting for us to reach out and claim his promises. Calling indicates that we need help and that we depend on One outside of ourselves. But we call not only on God, who is able, but we are instructed to call the "elders of the church." In New Testament times, elders were recognized as leaders in the congregation, not because of their age or elected position, but because of their consistent Christian lives and their spiritual maturity. The body of believers could place their confidence in them because these individuals were filled with the Holy Spirit and knew the power of prayer in meeting human need. Healing services are not for curiosity seekers or onlookers but for believing members of the household of faith.

The Holy Spirit also helps us to understand that there is no magical power in the oil used for anointing the sick. Though olive oil is commonly used, it is simply a symbol of the power of the Spirit in the act of healing. Anointing is not effective because of any magical quality of the oil or because of any supernatural power possessed by the person praying. Rather, anointing and praying over a sick person is effective because it is an act of obedience to the Word of God. And obedience is required for healing to be released.

Spiritual healing—conversion—is hindered many times by our failure to realize our need for reconciliation with God and with the one wronged. While salvation is not determined by such an act alone, the restoration is an indication of the experience received. Divine physical healing is not unlike this spiritual healing.

James, after giving clear directions as to how the sick may receive physical healing, adds this instruction, "Confess your faults to one another" (5:16, KJV). Healing is not determined by such confession, but it removes anything that may hinder the healing of body and spirit. Our Helper, the Holy Spirit, calls to mind those things that should be confessed and to whom. Confession ordinarily is not made publicly to all. Confession of doubt, anger, jealousy, fear, broken relationships has many times removed barriers to physical healing. Prayer is confession to God, and such believing prayer is experienced in healing.

Two benefits result from this prayer: restored health and forgiveness. Neither the length of the prayer nor the human status of the one praying is important. What matters is that the prayer is offered out of the faith and fervency of a Spirit-filled life. "The prayer of a righteous man is powerful and effective" (James 5:16).

Helps to Health

Holiness helps us to realize the truth contained in Bruce Larson's book titled *There Is a Lot More to Health Than Not Being Sick.* Larson says that in our search for relief from sickness, we must not allow our spiritual, emotional, and physical health to weaken. Life experience provides evidence of the connection between health and negative emotional states, such as loneliness, fear, hopelessness, resentment, jealousy, envy, stress, anxiety, anger, and lack of purpose. Our feelings about ourselves and others exert more influence on our health than genes, chemistry, or environmental factors. Physical healing often requires inner healing first. The illuminating presence of the Holy Spirit makes us aware of this need for inner healing of all facets of our being—emotions, attitudes, and relationships.

Spiritual Obedience

Sanctification is an inner work of grace. It involves much more than our actions, behavior, and deeds. It deals with our reactions, our beliefs, and our dispositions. The experience of holiness, living in the Spirit, enables us to "keep in step with the Spirit" (Gal 5:25). Eugene Peterson calls living in the Spirit a "long obedience in the same direction."[1] One may be physically limited in body but still maintain a healthy, radiant, positive spiritual attitude. Paul, though infirm in body and never healed, could say, "Be joyful always" (1 Thess 5:16).

Our Helper is our guide to survival. He calls to mind God's Word, which says, "Be still, and know that I am God" (Ps 46:10). It is very difficult in a world of cell phones, computers, and television to quiet our souls and listen for the still small voice of God. For most of us to hear his voice, God would have to shout to get our attention. The Holy Spirit is gentle: He never knocks down the closed door of your heart or mind, but he always waits for you to hear God's voice. When we take time to listen, we come to an awareness that in this Spirit-filled life, each of us has a responsibility to "purify ourselves from everything that contaminates body and spirit" (2 Cor 7:1). Such soul-cleansing experiences do not come eas-

---

[2]Peterson, *A Long Obedience.*

ily. We find it difficult to have even a little space in daily living, a time to be by ourselves, for meditation and listening to God.

Though we cannot isolate ourselves from the reality of the world as the desert fathers did, it is possible for us to pray, "Search me, O God, and know my heart" (Ps 139:23). As we do so, a cleansing comes through the Word of God (Eph 5:26) as truth is revealed to us by the Holy Spirit. Then in the worship services of the church, the community of faith, we have opportunity to celebrate this discipleship with other believers.

Spiritual obedience enables us to experience victory even when we are challenged by sickness and suffering.

Think on These Things

Mental health, how we think and what we allow to infiltrate our minds, has great bearing on our physical well-being. Almost imperceptibly, our thoughts are shaped by the media: what we see, hear, read, or listen to subconsciously. Though we may think that we are not listening or looking, our minds still process the sights and sounds that surround us. Like incipient decay, the values and mores of society shape how we feel and what we believe. It is true: We are not what we think we are; but what we *think*, we *are*! No doubt that is why the Holy Spirit helps us understand Paul's words, "Our battle...is to take every thought captive to obey Christ" (2 Cor 10:5).

Bringing our attitudes and our thought processes under the control of the Spirit is not easy. Only the Holy Spirit can enable us to escape from the narcissism and self-assertiveness that has become the acceptable standard, even within the church. Inordinate pride, self-centeredness, self-will, egotistic self-esteem, and self-approbation must all be brought into submission to Christ. Though infirm in body, Paul could say, "For my part, I am going to boast about nothing but the Cross of our Master, Jesus Christ. Because of that Cross, I have been crucified in relation to the world, set free from the stifling atmosphere of pleasing others and fitting into the little patterns that they dictate" (Gal 6:14, MSG). Paul describes the key to positive mental health in Philippians 4:8: "You'll do best by filling your minds and meditating on things true, noble, reputable, authentic, compelling, gracious—the best, not the worst; the beautiful, not the ugly; things to praise, not things to curse" (Phil 4:8, MSG).

Disciplined Discipleship

Holiness helps us to make healthy decisions—decisions that take the long look, that consider the cost, and that make a commitment to pay the price to reach the goal. This generation does not know the meaning of delayed gratification. We want everything today, not tomorrow. This attitude has affected all of society: big business, professional athletics, and church growth. We have forgotten this basic biblical truth: "He who stands firm to the end will be saved" (Matt 10:22). We do not become holy by just praying at an altar; we become holy by living a faithful life of dedicated discipleship.

We want healthy bodies without having to practice the discipline of good health. The term *workaholic* defines our culture. We fail to recognize that we are stewards of our bodies and that we will be held accountable for the way we treat them (1 Cor 6:19–20). God cannot help our infirmities if we persist in destroying the bodies in which we live.

Our Helper, the Holy Spirit, reminds us that good health is made possible by self-discipline, proper rest, healthful diet, and exercise on a consistent basis. It cannot be purchased at a health store. God's Word is not a diet book, nor is the Holy Spirit your personal trainer; but together they will help you experience abundant life even when you are physically challenged. The self-discipline required will not make you holy, but a holy life in the Spirit is a disciplined life.

When Healing Doesn't Come

If we have obediently done all that Scripture requires, what do we do when healing does not come? The question is valid and it deserves an answer. Often, the answers given are insufficient—answers such as "There is some sin in your life" or "You do not have sufficient faith." Neither is necessarily true. Many people have been faithful servants of God—victorious over sin, the world, the flesh, and the devil—yet their prayers for healing went unanswered. This concern is accentuated when we pray for someone dear to us, particularly a child or companion, only to watch the loved one suffer and sometimes die. That tests our faith to the breaking point. Our Helper, the Holy Spirit, once again calls to our remembrance the Word of God.

Behold His Glory!

The struggle of the human soul in sorrow is revealed in the account of Mary, Martha, and Lazarus (John 11:1–45). Here was a loving family into which Jesus had been received and believed. And Jesus loved them, caring deeply about their lives and needs. In a time of sickness, they did as Scripture tells us to do: they called on the Lord (11:3). When Jesus did not respond immediately, they did not lose faith, but they did not understand: "If you had been here, my brother would not have died. But I know that even now…" (vv. 21–22).

When healing does not come, don't give up! God is still in control. Out of the darkness of death, Christ can bring the light of the resurrection. To Martha, Jesus said, "Did I not tell you that if you believed, you would see the glory of God?" (v. 40). When you or a loved one for whom you prayed is not healed, look for the glory of God to be revealed. The Westminster Catechism asks, "What is the chief end of man?" The answer, "To glorify God and enjoy Him forever."

Perfect His Strength

Have you asked repeatedly for God's healing touch, but your prayers have not been answered? Someone may say to you that prayer is always answered: sometimes God says, No; at other times, Grow; and then, Go. But when you are in pain, you have cried until you can cry no more, and prayer seems not to prevail, pat answers are of little consolation. But it is only then that we cast ourselves on the strength of God, when we have run out of answers and have no more strength.

At such times, we remember Paul's struggle with sickness. He repeatedly sought the Lord for healing, three times according to Scripture, but perhaps that only emphasizes for us the continuing anguish of his soul.

Paul did not give up. He kept on praying until the Lord said, "My grace is sufficient for you, for my power is made perfect in weakness" (2 Cor 12:9). This truth caused Paul to say, "I will boast…in my weaknesses." What was his weakness? Some say it was poor eyesight, perhaps glaucoma. Whatever his affliction, there was no healing; he suffered with it for life. Speaking of Paul, missionary E. Stanley Jones wrote, "When his eyesight went bad, his insight went better." No doubt that is the meaning of Andraé Crouch's lyrics: "If I'd never had a problem I wouldn't know that He could solve them, I'd never know what faith in God could do."[3]

Experience His Presence

God is experienced in the most unlikely places, many of which involve suffering and pain. Remember Moses in the desert, Daniel in the lions' den, the three Hebrew children in the fiery furnace, Paul and Silas in prison, and the stoning of Stephen. In the midst of painful circumstances, these people experienced the presence of God. When our prayers for healing are not answered and we hurt so much that we would like to escape

---

[3]"Through It All" by Andraé Crouch. In *Hymns for the Family of God*, 43.

it all, we can say with Jacob of old, "Surely the LORD is in this place, and I was not aware of it" (Gen 28:16). Healing does not come for everyone, but God comes to everyone. To everyone, he gives songs in the night and hope in despair. He is indeed a very present help in every time of need. Remember, you are not alone!

> O Love that will not let me go,
> I rest my weary soul in Thee;
> I give Thee back the life I owe,
> That in Thine ocean depths its flow
> May richer, fuller be.[4]

FOR FURTHER STUDY:

1. Why are faith and obedience necessary for healing?

2. How can suffering and sorrow be for the glory of God?

3. Why should we seek medical treatment when divine healing is taught in the Bible?

4. Are all healing methods acceptable to a Christian? What about healings where God, the church, or faith are not even considered? Explain your answer.

5. How do holiness of life and harmony within the life of the local congregation create an atmosphere of faith for divine healing?

6. How can Christian conduct and behavior—care of the body, good eating and rest habits, honest work ethics, time for vacation—serve as a guarantee against sickness and disease?

7. Do you believe that healing that comes through the process of waiting on God's good timing is as spiritual and real as that healing which is instantaneous or miraculous? Explain why.

---

[4]"O Love That Will Not Let Me Go" by George Matheson. In *Worship the Lord*, 453.

Be eager to remain *one* in the Spirit.
Be at peace with *one* another.
We who are in Christ ought to be *one*;
we are *one* body; there is only *one Holy Spirit*...

—EPHESIANS 4:3–4, LAUBACH

PURITY...UNITY... POLITY!

Swayed by the latest leadership technique in the popular press or by the success of the latest growing church down the street, some churches have become captive to defective church governance.

James R. Hawkinson & Robert K. Johnson
Servant Leadership, vi

12

Purity...Unity...Polity!

THE HOLY SPIRIT is involved in the total life of the church. Pentecost produced "the church which is his body" (Eph 1:22–23). Christ is the head of the Body and the Holy Spirit is the administrator, our "Lord's ever-present other self."[1] More than a humanly organized institution, the church is a living organism through which the Holy Spirit carries out God's purpose. Therefore, the Spirit is not only concerned about the spiritual, physical, and emotional aspects of our lives, but also about the relational and organizational functions of the Body, to which we belong. How the local church is organized or governed is a practical demonstration of our theology of the Holy Spirit.

Polity is the system by which a particular church or body governs itself or is governed. Every church has a polity, either written or unwritten. It is the manner by which each local church administers its programs and sustains its members. Using the metaphor of a body with many parts (or members), Paul emphasizes that regardless of the number of individuals in the church, there is only one Spirit (Eph 4:4). While some have questioned organizing the work of the church, a church body that is not properly structured is severely limited in what it is able to do. Simply stated, when the Holy Spirit is not in control, the church is out of control.

Polity, governance, and administration—rightly perceived and faithfully practiced—can be a source of great blessing, setting legitimate boundaries and clearly establishing accountability and lines of responsibility. It is equally true, however, that when polity is exploited for personal ambition,

---

[1]Wiley, *Christian Theology*, 311.

119

it can become destructive, causing division within the Body. This is often the result of giving authority and power to a particular person or select group without built-in controls for accountability to the Body.

Polity Helps People

Following the day of Pentecost, the expansion of the young church was both explosive and exciting, creating unanticipated demands upon the apostles. These followers of the Way had grown from the Twelve to seventy to one hundred and twenty, and then suddenly to three thousand. Church growth always presents challenges to church structure; many times, divine assistance is required to meet the human demands. When confronted by such a need, the apostles had to call on the Holy Spirit for both governance and administration. Acts 6:1–8 reveals how they were directed in evaluating the need, establishing requirements for personnel, and providing basic guidance for the church's administration. The need of their time and place determined the actual implementation of the polity. One of the keys to the success of the young church was the flexibility of their polity.

Regardless of the size of a congregation, fulfillment of the ministry of servanthood requires a functional spiritual polity in administering God's work. The Holy Spirit is the wind of God, moving many times in ways that we do not fully understand or control, but always to meet human need. In business, this is the principle that form follows function. In the life of the church, we might say that purpose determines polity. The church's supreme statement of purpose was given by Christ himself in Luke 19:10: "For the Son of Man came to seek and to save what was lost." Our polity, therefore, must reflect the purpose for which we exist, as revealed in Christ.

Polity Portrayed

Historically, polity has emerged repeatedly in three basic forms: episcopal, presbyterian, and congregational. I refer to these forms of church polity only briefly, acknowledging that the Holy Spirit has and does work in each form when the people are surrendered to his will.

Episcopal church government finds its roots in the New Testament Greek words *eppiscopos* (bishop) and *presbuteros* (elder). This type of polity vests power and authority within the church in the hands of bishops, elders, and deacons. Also included in this form of polity are the concepts of apostolic succession and the appointment of bishops over the church.

Presbyterian church polity has roots in the Protestant Reformation and finds support in the New Testament Greek word *presbyter* (elder). It seeks to establish a middle ground between the authoritarianism of episcopal church government and the independence of congregational autonomy. To do so, it allows members of the local church to exercise authority in the choice of officers and other related matters in congregational life.

Congregational church government is characterized by the autonomy of the local church, in which is vested the final authority, allowing voting and control by the local members. Inherent in this is the belief that Christ is the head of the Body (Col 1:18) and that the members share in the priesthood of all believers (1 Peter 2:5, 9). Spiritual oneness is the unifying force that holds congregations together voluntarily, rather than an imposed unity from denominational structure. Through a common loyalty to Christ, clergy and laity share together in ministry and outreach.

All three forms of polity involve basic biblical teachings and express a common faith. While all forms serve one Lord, their style of servanthood and service vary greatly. In his book *The Primitive Church*, B. H. Streeter has written:

> In the Primitive Church there was no single system of Church Order laid down by the Apostles. During the first hundred years of Christianity, the Church was an organism alive and growing… changing its organization to meet changing needs…no one system of Church Order prevailed.[2]

The early Christians relied upon the Holy Spirit to help them address and meet human need. No doubt that is why the writer of Revelation said repeatedly, "He who has an ear, let him hear what the Spirit says to the churches" (2:29).

Potential of Polity

Polity does not protect the church from problems, but it does present the potential for a positive resolution of them. It was through prayer and the inspiration of the Holy Spirit that the apostles prescribed a course of action that released the young church for continued growth (Acts 6:1–8). Holy Spirit administration in the church allowed for the involvement of all people and the implementation of their gifts. This vision was not cast by a single leader, but together those involved agreed upon an approach to meet the need. Though the plan was perceived by the apostles (Acts 6:2), they involved the people (6:3), and the whole body (6:5) together selected leaders to carry out the plan. With unanimous agreement on the

---

[2]Streeter, *Primitive Church*, 267.

selection, the individuals chosen were approved by the laying-on of hands and prayer. This laying-on of hands was not an investiture of power or office but an act of agreement that the Holy Spirit approved their action. Note that no orders were given, no demands were made, and no guilt trips were placed upon the participants. Participation was simply the result of humble submission to the Spirit in their midst. Godly governance within the church produces positive results. "So the word of God *spread*. The number of disciples in Jerusalem *increased rapidly*, and a *large number* of priests became obedient to the faith" (6:7). An added blessing was that Stephen, one of the "serving" group, began a preaching ministry (6:8). All of this occurred without bylaws being rewritten, a church growth conference, or even a committee meeting or seminar—only the leadership and anointing of the Holy Spirit.

Inherent in this example of polity is the recognition and use of gifts distributed by the Holy Spirit. Each spiritual gift in the church has been given for the "common good" (1 Cor 12:7). Paul gives a good polity principle for avoiding conflict over the importance of individuals or different gifts: "Don't cherish exaggerated ideas of yourself or your importance... for just as you have many members in your physical body and those members differ in their functions, so we, though many in number comprise one body in Christ and are all members one of another. Through the grace of God we have different gifts" (Rom 12:3–6, Phillips).

Properly understood, polity in the local congregation and the general offices of the church does not allow for special recognition or preferential treatment because of spiritual gifts, titles, or position. Our gifts may differ and our specific ministry may go unnoticed by those around us, but in God's kingdom each follower is vital, essential, and of equal importance. Church structure must always function as a means of allowing full expression of the Holy Spirit, recognizing and exercising the gifts of every member of the Body.

Perils of Polity

The word *peril* speaks of possible danger and vulnerability, of leaving oneself exposed. This was the condition of the young church in the book of Acts. Predominantly made up of people from Jewish background, the early church found a certain security in the law—how to act, what to give, and how to worship. Now that they had been set free in Christ from the structure of Judaism (Gal 5:1), they were in danger. Without experience in church governance, they were like infants (1 Peter 2:2), immature in the faith while contending with false teachers (2 Peter 2:1) who denied the Lordship of Christ.

Freedom in the Holy Spirit required that they exercise their liberty in making decisions, choosing whom to believe and follow. Yet there were many voices within the church, each endeavoring to exercise authority, sometimes with signs and wonders. There have always been those who, claiming the anointing of the Holy Spirit, intentionally or mistakenly exploit the polity of the church for their own ends. In so doing, they seriously impair the effectiveness of the body of Christ. The congregational type of polity, with its concept of congregational autonomy, is particularly susceptible to this problem; congregations with no accountability to the church at large can become the base of operation for these whom Peter called "false prophets and false teachers" (2 Peter 2:1). Although this assertion may be questioned by some, it has been validated and articulated by Ronald M. Enroth in his frightening book *Churches that Abuse*.[3] Addressing the issues of legalism, authoritarian leadership, manipulation, excessive discipline, and spiritual intimidation, Enroth highlights the peril of a polity that is not under the control of the Holy Spirit. Commenting on the book, Richard Pierard of Indiana State University, said, "Ron Enroth demonstrates convincingly that authoritarian preachers, who twist scriptures to pass themselves off as Spirit-filled men of God, unconscionably exploit the trust of sincere and credulous believers for their own selfish benefit."[4]

This peril is particularly true of church bodies that have elevated the authority of the preacher, using Scripture to justify their lack of accountability, even in ordination. Exploiting their autonomy, these congregations become a law unto themselves. Accountable to no one and guided by no doctrine, they set themselves apart from other Christians by exercising a special interpretation of Scripture that is claimed to be a special "word from the Lord."

Abandoning humble servanthood, many individuals and churches have sought, given, and used scriptural titles for leadership positions in a quest for authority, power, status, and control. The terms *bishop*, *elder*, and *deacon* are often improperly bestowed and inappropriately exercised. Biblically, they are intended for local use only, with little significance elsewhere. No titles were used in the Jerusalem Council (Acts 15), for example. And little consideration is given to the fact that Jesus instituted no

---

[3]Enroth, *Churches That Abuse*, Introduction.

[4]As quoted on the back jacket of Enroth, *Churches That Abuse*.

offices and gave no titles. Ignored is Jesus' admonition that "the greatest among you will be your servant" (Matt 23:11). In a push to excel and to grow as congregations, church leaders justify rewriting bylaws to allow for maximum freedom in exercising control of the flock over which the Holy Spirit has made them overseers (Acts 20:28). Such actions allow us to build our own little kingdoms; we appoint individuals who support our style of leadership and place total control of the congregation under one church "CEO," displacing the Holy Spirit.

Again, church polity developed under the leadership of the Holy Spirit will not prevent problems, but it will help us preserve the ministry of the Holy Spirit and the unity of the congregation.

Unity

Unity among the followers of Christ is the product of the purity of the heart and is thus not guaranteed by church polity. Church creeds, disciplines, catechisms, and formal membership may bring people together in a common endeavor, but they will not of themselves unite the people. The scriptural model of Christian unity was established by Jesus when he prayed for the disciples, "For their sakes I sanctify Myself, that they themselves also may be sanctified in truth" (John 17:19, NASB). Explanation of his desire is expressed in verse 21: "...that they [the disciples] may be one; even as You, Father, are in Me, and I in You...that the world may believe..." (NASB). The unity Christ desired for the church can only be found when believers follow him as the Head of the church.

It is this high calling to which every believer is called: to be united in Christ, to each other, and to the truth (Eph 4:13). Biblical unity is not organizational or institutional but relational. It is a unity in which individuals from diverse backgrounds and theological teachings have through a common faith in Christ been placed in the body of his church, enabling us to live together in harmony as the family of God. Little formal governance (polity), as we know it, is needed in a Spirit-filled and Spirit-led church. Perhaps that is why governance is so briefly mentioned in the New Testament.

The unity for which Christ prayed finds its most adequate expression "in a community characterized by shalom (peace, wholeness)."[5] Such peace is maintained by an inner awareness that without humility, gentleness, forbearance, and love (Eph 4:2), there can be no unity. Paul's belief in the necessity of the Spirit's grace in the church is evidenced by his identifica-

---

[5]Fee, *God's Empowering Presence*, 700.

tion of four fruit of the Spirit (Gal 5) as basic to Christian unity. Only an inner spirit of love, not a written polity, will enable us to acknowledge our diversity and accept one another as Christ has accepted us. Only love, the fruit of the Spirit, can prevent the rivalry, alienation, and division that weaken the witness of the Body.

The church is credible only when it stands united. Is it not possible for members of the Household of Faith to have wide diversity in worship styles, spiritual gifts, and polity without allowing these things to break the unity of the Spirit? Do we not believe that the presence of the Holy Spirit in our lives and in our churches gives us the power to rise above petty jealousies, competition, and exploitative manipulation?

Rising above such human weaknesses demands spiritual maturity in Christ (Eph 4:13). Maturity implies a process of growing up. Holiness of heart is not a state that we grow into; but living a life of holiness requires that we grow, for otherwise we die. Maturity does not mean that we have arrived, but rather that our childish ways will no longer control our lives since "we will no longer be infants" (Eph 4:14). When we are spiritually immature, we tend to be overly impressed with each new novelty because we lack the stability of spiritual discipline; we are tossed back and forth by our childish whims from one new thing to the next (Eph 4:14). Paul said, "When I became a man [mature], I put childish things behind me" (1 Cor 13:11). Marks of Christian maturity include the ability to accept responsibility, to make critical decisions, to work cooperatively with others, and to practice the disciplines of the Spirit.

It is true that some things involved in growing up spiritually can become seeds of division within the Body. In the first-century church, it was the struggle to accept the diversity of gifts. Which gifts are most important? Should followers of Christ prefer gifts that are more highly visible, those drawing greater attention? To be able to accept with grace those more gifted than ourselves is a mark of Christian maturity.

And what of the need to discern the divine from the human when someone claims to be speaking for God? As mature Christians, we will be called upon to make decisions that require the ability to forget about ourselves and focus on God's will for his people. In such situations, Paul says that "speaking the truth in love, we are to *grow* up...into Christ" (Eph 4:15, RSV). There will be times when a majority vote does not make an action right. At such times, maturity requires that we take a stand in love, seeking God's guidance and approval.

Polity is only the organizational structure within which we carry out the work of the church. Christian unity—the church united in Christ and directed by the Holy Spirit—is the source from which our polity emerges. Without true unity in Christ, our polity is pointless.

Purity

John R. Stott, noted British scholar and pastor, comments on Ephesians 4: "Moral purity always precedes institutional unity."[6] Without purity of intent, there can be no true biblical unity regardless of the polity developed or the governance exercised. If the attitude of those producing the polity is not pure and positive, then that which is produced will make little difference in the life of the church. Polity grows out of the heart and soul of the congregation. "As a man [person] thinketh in his heart, so is he" (Prov 23:7, KJV). Polity springs from the deep desires of the heart, finding expression in the mind of the people of God. Paul counsels, "Be transformed by the renewing of your mind" (Rom 12:2). Pure and positive attitudes were expected and required of church leaders in the first-century church. Purity was and is the first priority; it is more important than popularity, possessions, political power, or even spiritual giftedness.

While sometimes confused with perfectionism, moral purity is purity of intent. It is the desire to "love the Lord your God with all your heart and with all your soul and with all your mind" (Matt 22:37). It was the norm of the New Testament church, those followers that Paul prayed would be sanctified, set apart, kept by God's grace (1 Thess 5:23). As a result of total consecration (Rom 12:1) on our part as believers, the Holy Spirit will sanctify our lives, equipping each of us for servanthood in the church.

Speaking of Jesus, John the baptizer said, "He shall baptize you with the Holy Ghost, and with fire" (Matt 3:11, KJV). This symbolism, visible on the day of Pentecost (Acts 2:3), reveals the cleansing aspect of the Spirit-filled life. It is the result of a hungering and thirsting after righteousness, of wanting more than anything else to be like Jesus, of a willingness to die to self.

> *Yielded to Thee, all my selfish desires*
> *Perished one day 'mid the Pentecost fires;*
> *Yielded to thee, now thy image shall be*
> *Stamped and engraven forever on me.*[7]

---

[6]Stott, "Studies in Ephesians."

[7]Verse 3 of "Yielded to Thee," by Haledor Lillenas. In *Hymnal of the Church of God*, 134.

When cleansed of all "selfish desires," church leaders are able to become oriented to servanthood. Moral purity leaves no room for egotistical, independent, authoritative, domineering control of the church. Rather than seeking the vision of a single leader or an official board, the Holy Spirit brings us together in a mature unity to achieve God's will (Gal 2:20). Such purity is evidenced not by the size of a church but by a sensitivity to the Holy Spirit, who always leads to greatness through servanthood. Christ, the Head of the church, set the example when he washed the disciples' feet (John 13) and took upon himself the form of a servant (Phil 2:7). He led by serving and submitting to the Father, asking that it happen "not as I will, but as you will" (Matt 26:39).

Biblical principles always take priority over established church polity. God's Word gives specific guidance about leadership requirements. Among many qualifications, an individual selected to lead is not to be a beginner in the faith (1 Tim 3:6). Spiritual maturity, or walking in the Spirit (Gal 5:25), is essential in preparation to serve. While life experience is valuable, it must always be tested against the Word of God. Without spiritual growth and maturity, we can fail to discern the guidance of the Holy Spirit. Paul, preaching in a "demonstration of the Spirit's power" (1 Cor 2:4), said, "The man without the Spirit does not accept [understand] the things that come from the Spirit of God, for they are foolishness to him, and he cannot understand them, because they are spiritually discerned" (1 Cor 2:14). Because of this, Jesus prepared the disciples with the assurance that "when he, the Spirit of truth, comes, he will guide you into all truth" (John 16:13).

How does one discern the right person to pastor a church? Or to direct a national church office? Or to serve on councils or committees? Or to formulate church budgets? Academic degrees, professional certifications, and success in the business world do not necessarily qualify one for leadership in the church. Only when such accomplishments are fully yielded to the Holy Spirit's control can they be useful in the Kingdom. It is through obedient holy living, walking in the light of God's Word, and seeking his face in prayer that one comes to understand and know the will of God.

The fruit of the Spirit is evidence of a pure heart. As outlined in previous chapters, this triad of Christian graces produces positive attitudes in the life of the church. Purity of heart enables us to grow in the likeness of Christ (Rom 8:9). In contrast to the works of the flesh (Gal 5:19–21), the fruit of the Spirit (moral purity) is characterized by a spiritual mind, by mature relational virtues, and by practical behavior.

New Testament unity was not the result of a religious document or legalistic governance, but of a people yielded to the Holy Spirit. Peter's Pentecostal sermon reveals that the disciples were no longer self-seeking or desiring places of power; they had been cleansed of pride, arrogance, and selfishness. We read that he preached "standing up *with the eleven*" (Acts 2:14). His eleven companions now became the supporting cast, holding Peter up in prayer as he preached. More than simply the excitement of the moment, this cooperative witness became the pattern of operation for the young church. Already cited is the example of Acts 6. Cooperative witness also appears in Acts 15 in the action of the Jerusalem Council. The decision reached and the action taken were not dictated by one authoritative person or by a written decree. The report reads, "It seemed good to the Holy Ghost and to us..." (15:28, KJV). The church reached no consensus without the blessing and agreement of the Holy Spirit.

Good polity requires patient understanding and willingness to relinquish our way for God's way. Impatience in the work of the church is an indicator of spiritual immaturity. Patience is always vital to the implementation of Spirit-led church polity. The bylaws may allow a simple majority (51 percent) to determine a decision, but that does not necessarily mean that such a decision is the right way to go. God is in no hurry! And according to Scripture, "Even Christ did not please himself" (Rom 15:3). Many Christians do not know the meaning of the phrase *delayed gratification*. Rather than waiting for congregational unity to be achieved by the Holy Spirit, we push through business motions and resolutions to gratify our own personal desires for a particular program. Healthy church life is the work of people unified by the awareness that in the fullness of time (Gal 4:4), God, not their vote, will bring things to pass.

Church polity should reflect the inclusiveness of the Body. Each spiritual gift given is to be exercised in the church regardless of the gender of the person. Social custom has too often been adopted in the church, thus disenfranchising women of their function in the Body. Our fear of words like *submission* and *authority* has seriously limited the role of women as leaders in the church. Inspired by the Holy Spirit, Paul wrote, "Gone is the distinction between Jew and Greek, slave and free man, *male and female*...you are all one in Christ!" (Gal 3:28, Phillips). Moral purity requires honesty, an honesty that acknowledges the giftedness of all Christians, men and women, and their rightful place of ministry in the church.

The polity developed by a Spirit-filled people will recognize that the Holy Spirit always has the final say on all issues pertaining to the life of the church. Before every meeting of the Body in which issues are to be considered, it should be our priority to seek to know God's will through prayer. Even before praying, we know that God's will is always for the common good, not for the good of just one individual; God's will is for that which "edifies the Body," not just a select group of people. We also know that the Holy Spirit has the power to veto any decision we have made. Paul and Timothy envisioned going to Asia to preach the gospel, but "they were kept by the Holy Spirit from preaching the word in the province of Asia" (Acts 16:6). The vision was cast and they had committed themselves, but the Holy Spirit said, No! It is a wise people whose polity is flexible enough to recognize that God has the final word even when they are already in process.

Included in the Bible's portrayal of Spirit-controlled, Spirit-governed people is the maturity to agree to disagree while still loving God, the church, and one another. Church polity, Christian unity, and heart purity do not mean that we will always have unanimity or that we will all agree. Paul and Barnabas loved God and the church, but they still had a "sharp disagreement" (Acts 15:36–40). In the face of strong disagreement, these men did not leave the church, did not lose respect for one another, and did not even quit supporting the church financially. The reason? Because the love of God was poured into their hearts by the Holy Spirit (Rom 5:5).

The ultimate purpose of Jesus' prayer for his disciples in John 17 is found in verse 21: "that the world may believe." That too is the purpose of John's gospel: "These are written that you may believe" (20:31). Reaching our postmodern world will require a united body of mature believers who authenticate their faith by consistent holy living. It must come from more than proper polity; it must come from personal holiness.

FOR FURTHER STUDY:

1. Of the three types of church polity listed, which one do you feel is most biblical? Explain why.

2. Which type of polity best expresses the theology of your church? Does the theology of a church make any difference in its form of polity?

3. By whom and in what way was the present polity of your church selected? When? Has it been recently revised?

4. Are there trends in today's church growth movement that precipitate changes in church polity? If so, please describe those trends and the changes they bring.

5. How, and in what way, does moral purity affect the polity of the local church?

6. Is there a danger in attempting to blend two different types of church polity? For example, imagine what is involved in attempting to blend episcopal and congregational church government: What are the similarities? What are possible conflicts?

7. Should there be a uniform church polity for all congregations in a given church communion? Would this advance unity? How could it be accomplished?

8. Is there a section of your church polity that calls for accountability of leadership? If so, to whom are they accountable? Are ordained staff members accountable to a credentials committee? Should they be? If so, why?

9. Do you have elders and deacons in your congregation? If so, please explain their purpose and responsibilities. How are they selected, ratified, or appointed, and by whom? What are the benefits of such positions and titles?

10. What is the danger of not having a written and adopted polity? Are there areas of vulnerability when such does not exist? If so, explain.

And [Jesus] said…
"Receive the Holy Spirit."

—JOHN 20:22

RECEIVE
THE
HOLY SPIRIT

To receive *is to accept something given to us by another and which we make a part of ourselves.* Receiving *also implies that we are doing something self-consciously.* To "receive the Holy Spirit" *is to embrace God fully and completely.*

Laurence W. Wood
Truly Ourselves, Truly the Spirit's, 197
(emphasis added)

13

Receive the Holy Spirit

GOD HAS a Pentecostal experience for you! Don't become alarmed—I am not referring to one with all of the audiovisual effects of wind, fire, and tongues. But I do mean that there is a purifying, ventilating, and exhilarating experience that will be known to you when the Holy Spirit becomes the obsession of your life. Samuel Hines, beloved pastor and evangelist, said, "When the Holy Spirit becomes your obsession, then you become his possession." It is at that time that Pentecost comes to you personally. That is God's promise.

John's account of the postresurrection appearance of Christ (John 20:19–29) does two things: First, it is a witness to the victory over death. To anxious hearts shut in by fear behind closed doors, Jesus speaks words of peace (vv. 19, 21, 26). Second, it testifies that Jesus breathed on them, saying, "Receive the Holy Spirit" (v. 22). While this text has caused concern to many, it is helpfully illuminated by Joseph Mayfield:

> This bestowal of the Spirit is not the same as that described in Acts 2:4. The first took place while Jesus was with his disciples, the latter after his ascension into heaven. The former was a bestowal on disciples who were most certainly God's children (John 17:9), "an earnest," while the latter was "His manifest coming and permanent abiding in them by His representative, the Paraclete." The former was not the fulfillment of Jesus' promise concerning the coming of the Comforter (John 7:39; 16:7), but it was a real impartation, an earnest of Pentecost.[1]

---

[1]Earle, *Beacon Bible Commentary*, 232.

133

Jesus wanted to verify to these frightened followers the truth of his Word regarding empowerment for service. Picking up all the Jewish history that we have mentioned in our study, he speaks of the Spirit that would be theirs and ours.

> There is no doubt that when John spoke in this way, he was thinking back to the old story of the creation of man. There the writer says: "And the Lord God formed man of the dust of the ground, and breathed into his nostrils the breath of life; and man became a living soul" (Gen. 2:7). The coming of the Holy Spirit is like a new creation; it is like the wakening of life from the dead. When the Holy Spirit comes upon the Church she is reawakened and recreated for her task.[2]

Therefore, as Jesus prepared to send them forth to serve, even as the Father had sent him into the world, he impressed upon the disciples the need for the infilling of the Holy Spirit. Our ministry today is no less demanding, and it is because of this that we consider how to receive the Holy Spirit.

In chapters 14 through 16 of John's gospel, Jesus reveals the nature of the Paraclete, the Holy Spirit. But it is in John 17 that we find help in preparing ourselves to receive the Spirit into our present lives. Basic to our understanding in receiving the Holy Spirit is an attitude of humility, with the intent to glorify God (17:1–5). In prayer, Jesus reveals the character of those whom he desires to see filled with the Spirit. They are "not of the world" (17:6, 16, KJV), and they have "obeyed your word" (17:6) as they have accepted and believed in Christ. He wants them to have the fullness of joy that comes through sanctified living—a life set apart for the specific infilling by and use of the Spirit. Jesus did not want them to be taken out of the world, to live in isolation, or to pursue a monastic way of life. Life in the Spirit equips one to come to grips with daily living, to live "soberly, righteously, and godly, in this present world" (Titus 2:12, KJV). It was the Truth (John 17:7) to which they had been exposed that would bring them to this experience. Truth creates in us a desire to know more truth. Therefore, these who recognized Jesus as the "way and the *truth* and the life" (John 14:6) now want the Spirit of Truth to live in them. As their model, Jesus becomes the example of every true believer and "sanctifies himself" (17:19). He knew that only in this surrender of self and all that one desires could unity prevail among the community of faith. Therefore Jesus said, "Receive the Holy Spirit."

---

[2]Barclay, *Gospel of John*, Vol. 2, 318.

Get Set!

While God has given us an example of how we should prepare to receive the infilling of the Spirit, let us guard against establishing a uniform pattern for this reception of God's gift. We must not stereotype the Holy Spirit! William Greathouse has written, "There certainly is no uniform pattern to be found, although certain underlying principles are apparent in every instance where the Holy Spirit has come in His sanctifying fullness. But there is no quick and easy formula for the power of God; God cannot be manipulated by psychological technique."[3] One might also add that neither can we receive the fullness of the Spirit through some phenomenological ecstasy that is psychologically produced in religious experience. The Spirit of God is free and works as he wills; therefore, we must simply present ourselves to be filled. To do so will require open honesty and courage. Rather than making us content with our inward selves, this experience creates in us a deeper hunger for the holiness of God.

Let us emphasize again that the disciples for whom Jesus was praying and upon whom he breathed these words *were already born of the Spirit.* They had believed on him (John 17:8), but he wanted them to experience the fullness of the Spirit. Too much time has been spent in theological debate regarding two works of grace. To say that it is impossible for one to be saved and sanctified at the same time is to limit God in what he is able to do. God is able to do all things, and he is not limited by our interpretation of his revealed acts in Scripture. However, to ignore the obvious intent of this passage in John 20:22, given to obedient followers and believers in Christ, would be equally in error. We must recognize that there is a deeper experience in the Holy Spirit beyond the initial experience of conversion. As Myron Augsburger has so helpfully stated, "The concern is not a question of time, but a question of reality."[4]

Is your experience in Christ adequate for all that he has called you to do? Or do you need more of his likeness in your life? Paul, speaking to the Ephesians, asked simply, "Did you receive the Holy Spirit when you believed?" (Acts 19:2). To receive him in his fullness, we should observe three underlying principles:

1. There must be an initial experience of personal belief in Christ.

---

[3]Greathouse, *Fullness of the Spirit*, 96.
[4]Augsburger, *Quench Not the Spirit*, 2.

2. Through Scripture, to which we respond in obedience, we hunger after more of God.

3. Within the heart and life of the individual believer, God has placed an awareness of greater dependence on him.

Go!

Having acknowledged this hunger for the righteousness of God, we should not postpone going boldly to the Father to receive his promised gift. It will require a decisive act on your part to ask for what is rightfully yours as a child of God. Samuel Chadwick wrote regarding this decisive act to receive the fullness of the Spirit: "There is a perfection that is definite, decisive, and determinate and there is a perfection that is progressive, disciplinary, and ethical; and there is an experience by which believers passed from one order to another."[5] Because of the semantic problem that many people have with the word *perfection*, I would like to restate what has just been quoted, using these words: "*an experience in the Holy Spirit* that is definite, decisive, and determinate; and there is *an experience in the Holy Spirit* that is progressive, disciplinary, and ethical; and there is an experience by which the believers passed from one order to another." This change does not alter Chadwick's original meaning, but it does help many people who are prone to interpret the word *perfection* in its ultimate sense, leaving absolutely no room for any further improvement nor allowing for any possibility of spiritual separation from God.

To experience the infilling of the Holy Spirit in your own life, you must ask for it openly and humbly. You should also check your underlying motives. Why do you desire to be filled with the Spirit? To seek such a blessing for personal reasons, such as desire for prestige, power, or spiritual success—no matter how legitimate you attempt to make them—will only lead to failure.

But having crucified the selfish ego, boldly ask for the Holy Spirit as we are instructed in Luke 11:13, "If you then, though you are evil, know how to give good gifts to your children, how much more will your Father in heaven give the Holy Spirit to those who *ask* him!" Then openly claim by faith what God has promised. Step out confidently, courageously, and expectantly into this new dimension of your experience in Christ. In complete reliance on him, allow your total life to be used for his glory. Do not

---

[5] Chadwick, *Way to Pentecost*, 106.

expect some meteoric climb to super sainthood or super church growth. All that the Holy Spirit imparts will be in balance, demonstrating an attractive Christian witness as you walk in the "highway of holiness."

How will you know that you are really filled with the Holy Spirit? The best way is begin with the basics. Seek Christ and know that you first belong to him. Then affirm in your own heart that you have opened yourself, asking for the Holy Spirit to fill your life. Believing that God has done exactly as he promised, you can anticipate the fruit of the Spirit in your attitudes.

Gifts do not necessarily prove that you have been filled with the Spirit; so check to see if the fruit of love, joy, and peace are produced in your daily life. You will also discover that God's Word will bear witness with your own heart that the Comforter abides within. And there will be peace, harmony, and unity that could come from nowhere else than a personal experience of Pentecost in your soul.

FOR FURTHER STUDY:

1. In what way is the Holy Spirit involved in the experience of conversion?

2. If we are born of the Spirit as described in John 3:5–6, what takes place when we receive the Holy Spirit?

3. What is the relationship between the two terms *salvation* and *sanctification*?

4. Does the infilling of the Holy Spirit make us perfect? Consider the implications of such terminology in our theology. If *perfection* is a good word, are we perfect humanly or spiritually?

5. Would you define the receiving of the Holy Spirit as a "definite crisis" experience? Support your response with Scripture.

6. Is it possible for one to sin after being filled with the Holy Spirit?

7. How would you explain to someone else the biblical teaching of the Spirit-filled life?

Quench not the Spirit.

—1 Thessalonians 5:19, KJV

QUENCH NOT
THE SPIRIT

The Holy Spirit *is working to bring our entire personality into conformity with His holiness. When we retain attitude, action, or appearance that is inconsistent with the mind of Christ, we are not sinning merely against the church, creed, or custom, but against the Spirit of Christ.*

Myron S. Augsburger
Quench Not the Spirit, 29
(emphasis added)

14

Quench Not the Spirit

SPIRITUAL SENSITIVITY is not fully developed at the time we are filled with the Holy Spirit. The graces received through his abiding presence (Gal 5:22–23) enable one to become more sensitive to God. There is the deepening awareness that the Holy Spirit is a person—living, thinking, seeing, hearing, and feeling.

One can almost see this developing in the life of Paul. When he was under the law, he was legalistic, stern, demanding, and even destructive. But in Christ, a glorious transformation begins to take place. Because of this change, Paul exclaims, "Where sin increased, grace increased all the more" (Rom 5:20). He was no less adamant in proclaiming God's expectation of holiness, but now he was "speaking the truth in love" (Eph 4:15).

Only one word adequately describes this Pauline experience in the Spirit; the word is *yieldedness*. Paul's life was totally yielded to the Spirit's control. His dedication was complete, his devotion constant, and his deeds consistent with a life of yieldedness. Wherever the Spirit led, Paul would go. Whatever the Spirit commanded, Paul would speak. And when the Lord wanted him to wait, Paul would stand still, waiting for divine direction. It was the kind of yieldedness that all of us must experience if we are to know the abundance of the Spirit-filled life.

Walking daily in the Spirit, Paul came to understand that there are ways of hindering the ministry of the Spirit. Three terms are used in Scripture to describe our human reactions to the Spirit's leadership. We will deal mainly with quenching the Spirit, but first let us look at all three terms together:

"You always *resist* the Holy Spirit!" (Acts 7:51).

"And do not *grieve* the Holy Spirit of God" (Eph 4:30).

"Do not *quench* the Spirit" (1 Thess 5:19, NASB).

G. Campbell Morgan refers to these as the perils of the Spirit-filled life. "The peril of *resisting* the Spirit is that of those who are not born again; the peril of *grieving* the Spirit is that of those who, born of the Spirit, are indwelt by Him; the peril of *quenching* the Spirit is that of those upon whom he has bestowed some gift for service."[1]

To *resist* implies an open rejection of the imploring Spirit that calls us to Christ. To *grieve* the Spirit means to bring sorrow to One who in gentleness and patience seeks to help us. He is grieved when we do anything that would detract from his holiness, for we are to be holy, even as he is holy (1 Peter 1:16). But to *quench* the Spirit is a problem that relates more to those who have received the infilling of the Holy Spirit, those who have become the "temple" of the Holy Ghost (1 Cor 6:19). This sensitive Spirit reigning within us can be quenched. The word means "to suppress, or to stifle." John F. Walvoord writes, "Quenching the Spirit may be simply defined as being unyielded to Him, or saying, 'No.' The issue is, therefore, the question of willingness to do His will."[2]

Some Ways of Quenching the Spirit

A. *Failure to heed the promptings of the Spirit.* "For God did not give us a spirit of timidity, but a spirit of power, of love and of self-discipline" (2 Tim 1:7). When we have been made aware of the leadings of the Holy Spirit but we fail to obey due to fear of what others may say, we quench the Spirit. Humble obedience to speak, serve, or remain silent as the Spirit directs is the yieldedness of sanctification.

B. *Bondage of individuals or the congregation in the worship of God will quench the Spirit.* There is a freedom that exceeds our humanly planned services of worship. If we will only allow him to, the Holy Spirit will be a participant in every service of worship. Dr. Harold Ockenga, in writing about the worship referred to in 1 Corinthians 14:33ff., comments:

> The Holy Spirit's direction played a very important part in the meetings of worship in the church. There was to be no restraint upon those who were guided by the Spirit in the midst of the worship. Here we are to avoid two extremes: One is the reaction against formalism which gives reign to extremes in the attempts

---

[1]Morgan, *Spirit of God*, 228.

[2]Walvoord, *Holy Spirit*, 197.

of people to follow the Spirit. This repels sincere and cultured persons. On the other hand, there is the impetus to quench all such individual expressions and to resort to a set form of service. Even the Holy Spirit could not break through some of these forms of service in our churches. It was the intention of Paul to maintain a nice balance between order and opportunity for the Spirit to work. The manifestations of the Spirit's working are not to be despised, nor are they to be courted.[3]

C. *Bitterness in attitude will quench the Spirit.* The nature of the Spirit is one of peace, joy, and love. Any attitude that would tend toward harsh, critical, or judgmental feelings are cautioned against in Scripture. "Make every effort to live in peace with all men and to be holy; without holiness no one will see the Lord. See to it that no one misses the grace of God and that no bitter root grows up to cause trouble and defile many" (Heb 12:14–15). The word translated *bitterness* has as its root meaning "a poisonous herb." As applied in the text, it is contrary to the nature of the Spirit and has a blighting effect upon his presence.

God is love. He has recreated us in his image through the Spirit and we are to be examples of love. This leaves no room for rancor, ill will, enmity, jealousy, or strife. Too often the Holy Spirit has been stifled by an ugly attitude expressed among people within the church.

D. *The Holy Spirit is not a fanatic, and we stifle true spirituality whenever we allow excesses to hinder his witness.* Samuel Shoemaker, Episcopalian servant of God, has written, "Let us beware of fanaticism. Faith in the Holy Spirit, even the beginnings of a true experience in Him, can be the occasion for the old ego to reassert itself. We can think we are guided in directions which prove in the end to be false, and we can be pushed by the uprush of the subconscious energies in directions that manifest more of self than of God."[4]

Whether one's witness manifests itself in noise or silence, laughter or weeping, leaping or sedentary worship—if it is of the Spirit, it will be done "in a fitting and orderly way" (1 Cor 14:40).

E. *Selfish pride will also grieve the Holy Spirit.* I qualify the type of pride, for pride can be either good or bad. A healthy sense of spiritual pride is needed in the Christian life. False, pretentious humility is no credit to God or his church. But pride that becomes excessive and carnal is evi-

---

[3]As quoted in Sanders, *Holy Spirit and His Gifts*, 97.

[4]Shoemaker, *With the Holy Spirit and with Fire*, 125.

denced by an unwillingness to admit human error or an insistence on our part that God has infallibly guided us in everything we have done. Tragic is the fact that the Holy Spirit has been blamed for a lot of human errors, simply because we have been too proud to admit we have been wrong.

While there are many other ways of quenching the Holy Spirit, these will help to guide us in avoiding anything that would suppress his will in our lives. It is possible to so resist, grieve, and quench the Spirit that we no longer sense his presence or hear his voice. Jesus referred to this as blasphemy against the Holy Spirit (Matt 12:31–32; Mark 3:28–29). It is a gradual process as we stifle the working of the Spirit in our lives. Stubbornness replaces yieldedness, callousness replaces compassion, and self usurps the place of the Spirit. Rather than surrendering, we quench his counsel. Rather than obeying him, we grieve him by ignoring God's call. In such manner as becomes his nature, the Holy Spirit quietly withdraws, not desiring to coerce or force us to respond. In this self-imposed sinful condition, we become insensitive to sin, unable to discern right from wrong, because the Holy Spirit, the convictor, has been quenched.

While some refer to this as the "unpardonable sin," it should be remembered that it is so called not because of God's unwillingness to forgive but because of our continued unwillingness to respond to the conviction of the Holy Spirit. In resisting him so long, we are deluded into believing that right is wrong and wrong is right—we are not able to discern truth, and therefore we do not seek him who is truth incarnate. Leslie Weatherhead has said, "If I were asked for a definition of the unpardonable sin, I would say that it is the sin of so continuously calling good evil, that the power of discrimination is killed and therefore the power to repent and to flee from sin is lost. The hunger for God is inhibited. The soul cannot respond to light, for it knows no difference between light and darkness."[5]

This is what transpires in the life of the child of God or the people of God who continually and persistently quench the Spirit. It is caused by our failure to serve him as he has endowed us with his power; our failure to praise him when he has filled us with joy; and our failure to seek him when he has given to us guidance and counsel. O Church of God, we dare not quench the Spirit! In an hour when there is a tendency to substitute human organization for divine revelation, when we are prone to depend on education rather than Holy Spirit inspiration, and when apostasy has become the accepted practice for many—let us remain sensitive to the Holy Spirit! Allow the Bible to remain the foundation of our faith, as the

---

[5]Weatherhead, *When the Lamp Flickers*, 48.

Spirit of Truth reveals God's message of love! Let the fire of Pentecost burn upon the altar of the church, consuming anything in our lives that would hinder his working in our midst! And pray that we would place our lives upon the altar of sacrifice, yielded to the Spirit's control.

> *Is your all on the altar of sacrifice laid?*
> *Your heart does the Spirit control?*
> *You will surely be blest and have peace and sweet rest,*
> *As you yield Him your body and soul.*[6]

FOR FURTHER STUDY:

1. Define the implications of the teaching that the Holy Spirit is a person.

2. Study the scriptural context in which Paul used the terms *grieve* and *quench* as relating to the Holy Spirit. Would you agree that the two terms refer to different degrees of offending the Spirit? How would you interpret the passages?

3. Do we quench the Spirit when we intentionally fail to produce the fruit of the Spirit?

4. How can one know when one has quenched the Spirit?

5. What is the difference between quenching the Spirit and committing a sin?

---

[6]Refrain, "Is Your All on the Altar?", by Elisha Hoffman. In *Worship the Lord*, 471.

Now unto him that is able to do
exceedingly abundantly above all
that we ask or think, according to the
power that worketh in us.

—EPHESIANS 3:20, KJV

THE ADEQUACY
OF THE
HOLY SPIRIT

Spirit-filled Christians know that to have the Spirit is to have all, for
everything He is and has is offered to us. The limitations are on our part,
for our capacity to understand and receive is restricted. As we set our
minds upon Him, the Spirit who dwells within us *gives us everything*
we need to meet anything that comes to us in our everyday living.

D. Shelby Corlett
God in the Present Tense, 147
(emphasis added)

15

The Adequacy of the Holy Spirit

PROOF OF THE HOLY SPIRIT is the persistence of the Christian church across the centuries. Persecution, apostasy, formality, liberalism, and other forms of opposition have never been able to silence the pulpits or close the doors of the church. One has only to recall the periodic outbreak of revival, which we can trace back to the working of the Holy Spirit. In the darkened catacombs of ancient Rome, the light of truth burned brightly. In the midst of a perverse and degenerate world, the cleansing fires of purity have burned in the lives of God's people. And with each succeeding generation, God has raised up a faithful remnant of his people, filled with his Spirit to be God's church in the world.

But it all began at Pentecost, the inauguration of the church—a time when men and women humbled themselves in prayer, yielded themselves to God, and were filled with the Holy Spirit. All of the things they experienced—the unity of believers, the production of spiritual fruit, the bestowal of gifts—were made possible because of the adequacy of *the Spirit*.

Adequate means "to be equal to what is required" or "fully sufficient." Paul could never escape the reality that God would do just as he had promised. Recall Paul's prayer that his Thessalonian friends become entirely sanctified. The passage is followed by these words: "The one who calls you is faithful and he will do it" (1 Thess 5:24). And Paul reveals this confidence as he prays for the Ephesians, "Now to him who is able to do immeasurably more than all we ask or imagine, according to his power that is at work within us, to him be glory in the church" (Eph 3:20–21).

The glory of the church past, present, and future is to be found in the adequacy of the Holy Spirit. He alone is able to provide our every need and equip us to fulfill God's purpose for our lives.

Without Him We Cannot Rightly Pray

No congregation is stronger than its prayer life. It is the lifeline that connects us with the eternal resources of an almighty God. Prayer produces the atmosphere that is conducive to the life and work of the Spirit.

But it is only through him that we can pray as we should. It is not that we are indifferent to prayer, but the deep yearnings of the soul are so many times beyond expression. Therefore God has given us what is adequate to the need. "We do not know what we ought to pray for, but the Spirit himself intercedes for us with groans that words cannot express" (Rom 8:26). There is no connection between this passage and the so-called modern "prayer language." Paul is merely emphasizing that, beyond what we can express in verbalized prayer, the Holy Spirit carries an even greater burden, and he expresses it in our behalf. Here is the divine Paraclete—the Comforter, Counselor, and Guide—interceding in our behalf.

Oh, that the Holy Spirit would raise up men and women of prayer within the church! It is only when supported by persistent prayer that our programs and preaching will succeed. Across the years, those who have left imprints upon the history of the church have been those known for their prayer life. Pentecost began in an Upper Room, where prayer was to be made. And if we are to serve our present age, the words of Jude must be observed, "Building up yourselves on your most holy faith, praying in the Holy Ghost" (v. 20, kjv). That is the key to unlocking the adequacy of the Holy Spirit—a prayer life like that of Jean-Nicolas Grou, who in the year 1750 prayed:

> O my Saviour, I say to Thee again with more insistence than ever: Teach me to pray; implant in me all the dispositions needful for the prayer of the Holy Spirit. Make me humble, simple and docile; may I do all that is in my own power to become so. Of what use is my prayer if the Holy Spirit does not pray with me? Come, Holy Spirit, come to dwell and work within me! Take possession of my understanding and of my will; govern my actions not only at the moment of prayer but at every moment. I cannot glorify God nor sanctify myself save by Thee.[1]

---

[1] Quoted in Ravenhill, *Revival Praying*, 62.

He Alone Is Adequate for Preaching

Pentecost produced preachers! They were ordinary people possessed by an extraordinary Spirit, who enabled them to witness to the resurrected Christ. Peter stood up and began to speak (Acts 2:14)—that's the simple statement of the dynamic beginning of this missionary enterprise that has swept across the world. Spirit-anointed preaching has made the difference.

In Acts 4:2, Peter and John are accused of preaching, but something went beyond their native ability in communicating with people. Verse 13 of that chapter reads, "They took note that these men had been with Jesus." The world was not convinced by their sophistication, erudition, or their oratorical eloquence. There was an adequacy in the Holy Spirit that more than compensated for their lack of all these human accomplishments. In no way does this lessen the importance of quality education and cultured refinement; it only highlights the positive fact that the Holy Spirit magnifies and enhances for God's glory whatever we yield to God.

Preaching is vital, for "God was pleased through the foolishness of what was preached to save those who believe" (1 Cor 1:21). However, to preach without the anointing of the Holy Spirit is to be "of all men most miserable." The essentiality of his blessing is amplified in the ministry of Christ, who opened his earthly ministry with the words of Isaiah 61:1–2: "The Spirit of the Lord is on me, because he has anointed me to preach good news…" (Luke 4:18). To attempt to preach without the unction of the Spirit is to do so at your own risk, which can have serious effect upon the worship of the community of faith. While some are concerned about the place of preaching in today's church, we need to be reminded that God's plan has not changed. Preachers are still called, and the Word is still being proclaimed—what is lacking is the anointing of the Holy Spirit.

How tragic if we have failed to inform the minister in Bible college or seminary that the Holy Spirit is indispensable in preaching! Without the anointing of the Spirit, sermon manuscripts became nothing more than well-written reports, and spoken words become only human speeches. Without his power, the message falls on unreceptive ears. Preaching requires anointed preachers who have been called of God, illuminated by the Spirit in the study of the Word, warmed by the Spirit in prayer, and inspired by the Spirit in the delivery of the message. The preacher does not touch the human heart; rather the Word of God comes alive when blessed of the Holy Ghost. As the followers of Karl Barth maintain, Scripture becomes the Word of God when the Spirit uses the Word preached or read to create an encounter with human hearts.

Paul expresses our dependence upon the Spirit as he writes to the Corinthians: "My message and my preaching were not with wise and persuasive words, but with a demonstration of the Spirit's power" (1 Cor 2:4). Wherever the Holy Spirit is, there is sufficient power to do God's will. It is not the volume of the voice but the holiness of the heart that makes the difference in preaching. God does not intend for us to live in the past or on experiences of the past. He has made possible through his Spirit a present experience that will equip us for the preaching and teaching of the Word. There is a fresh anointing for every worship service if preachers will only seek to surrender themselves to be used of him.

Receive the Holy Spirit—Then Witness!

This is the day of do-it-yourself evangelism. Almost every religious group has developed a four- or five-step plan to quick-and-easy soul winning. They provide a kind of self-training kit for evangelists.

Now, lest someone think I am making light of such programs, let me express my thanks for them. Anyone who believes the Bible should be extremely grateful for those whom God has used to develop means of leading persons to Christ. To believe the Bible implies that we also believe what it says about sin and judgment and being eternally lost without Christ. This frightening awareness should make all of us desire to bring others to Christ.

However, in spite of my gratitude for the programs of evangelism, Jesus said that we are not even to attempt to save the world until we have been filled with the Holy Spirit. The reasons are obvious. Only the Holy Spirit can open our understanding to sinfulness and God's plan of salvation. He alone is able to give spiritual birth to the person confessing sin. Without the Holy Spirit, we will miserably fail in reaching the unsaved. While we may know the right scriptures and how to share them winsomely with all of the proper illustrations, it is the work of the Holy Spirit that brings a decision to reality. Evangelism rather than some other charismatic enduement is the truest testimony of the Spirit-filled life. We are constrained to share God's love with those who have never come to know him. It will not necessarily be a prepackaged program of evangelism; it may be a spontaneous sharing of what God has done for us.

The early church, filled with the Holy Spirit, went everywhere turning the world upside down for Christ (Acts 17:6). He not only inspired them to witness, but he also gave direction in the missionary endeavors, opening and closing doors as would be pleasing to God.

If the first-century church could be used of God in reaching their world, is it not possible that every generation could touch the world with God's truth? The Holy Spirit is still adequate and available if we will claim by faith what God has promised to all of his children. It is a matter of historical record that whenever the people of God have humbled themselves in prayer and sought the infilling of the Holy Spirit, God has inevitably led them to victory against sin. Such triumphant testimonies are still being heard from those who have dared to step out on the adequacy of the Holy Spirit's power. His power is available to all people who are possessed of but one desire: to be used of God.

The Spirit's Adequacy for the Future

Great concern for the future of the church is expressed by the people of God. While we may be able to anticipate what the future will bring, and while we may even seek to bring certain changes in the days that lie ahead, we are not able to discern all that God has in store. Questions arise about values that appear to have changed. We wonder whether the church is able to speak to the needs of such a rapidly changing society.

I pray that, as we have sought to understand the Holy Spirit, we have discovered that he is always leading the church. From the beginning of time, he has been equipping the people of God to be the victors over the future, not the victims of time and transition. Our survival, spiritually and socially, will require our dependence on the Holy Spirit as he fills the church with power for service. We can prepare for survival by seeking spiritual renewal within the church.

Let us begin with revival! The Holy Spirit is adequate for a true spiritual awakening during these days of theological turbulence—not merely a revival of emotional involvement, but a revival of deep spirituality that brings maturity in Christ. It should result in personal, cultural, and economic changes in our lives. Dr. F. B. Meyer once said, "There has never been a great revival without social and political reforms." God did not divide our evangelical camps into polarized groups dealing with so-called social and personal gospels. He gave one gospel that exalts Christ, transforms human hearts, and reforms society through transformed lives. The adequacy of the Spirit for revival is to be seen in the fact there is no future without him and there can be no revival without him.

Yes, the greatest need of the church is the infilling of the Holy Spirit. However, his coming must begin with individuals within the church who answer this question: Have you received the Holy Spirit since you believed? (cf. Acts 19:2). If you have not received God's promise for your life, I pray that you will discover the fullness of the Spirit-filled life and face the future with the assurance of ultimate victory in Christ.

Even so, come Lord Jesus. Amen!

FOR FURTHER STUDY:

1. What can we do to ensure a continued emphasis on the necessity of the Holy Spirit's baptism and holy living within the church?

2. How do we maintain a healthy spiritual balance between the maximum use of our human potential and our total dependence on the Holy Spirit?

3. How should we react to the different types of religious worship when each particular group or style claims to be "in" the Spirit?

4. Is there a conflict between human organization and Holy Spirit leadership? Is so, how do we resolve this conflict?

5. In what manner can preaching be made more effective in communicating the good news? Is it by the Holy Spirit alone, or is there a human discipline that must also be exercised?

6. Study the unifying influence of the Holy Spirit in Acts, and then apply that example in today's church. Is unity God's plan for the church? If so, why is it that we seem to be divided over our understanding of the Holy Spirit?

7. Establish a pattern of Bible study and prayer in which you seek to know and experience the Holy Spirit in your life each day.

BIBLIOGRAPHY

Bibliography

Anderson School of Theology. *We Believe.* Anderson, IN: Anderson School of Theology, 1979.

Augsburger, David W. *The Love-Fight.* Scottdale, PA: Herald Press, 1973.

Augsburger, Myron S. *Quench Not the Spirit.* Scottdale, PA: Herald Press, 1975.

Barclay, William. *Daily Celebration.* Waco, TX: Word Books, 1971.

————. *The Gospel of John,* Vol. 2. Philadelphia: Westminster Press, 1956.

————. *More New Testament Words.* New York: Harper and Brothers, 1958.

————. *The Promise of the Spirit.* Philadelphia: Westminster Press, 1960.

Blackwelder, Boyce W. *Letters from Paul: An Exegetical Translation.* Anderson, IN: Warner Press, 1971.

Boyd, Myron F., and Merne A. Harris, comps. *Projecting Our Heritage.* Kansas City, MO: Beacon Hill Press, 1969.

Brown, Charles Ewing. *The Meaning of Sanctification.* Anderson, IN: Warner Press, 1945.

Callen, Barry L. *Following the Light: Teachings, Testimonies, Trials and Triumphs of the Church of God Movement, Anderson.* Anderson, IN: Warner Press, 1996.

Carpenter, Eugene E. "The Handiwork of God in Natural Creation." In *A Contemporary Wesleyan Theology,* edited by Charles W. Carter. Grand Rapids, MI: Zondervan, 1983.

Carter, Charles W. *The Person and Ministry of the Holy Spirit.* Grand Rapids, MI: Baker Book House, 1974.

Cattell, E. L. *The Spirit of Holiness.* Kansas City, MO: Beacon Hill Press, 1977.

Chadwick, Samuel. *The Way to Pentecost.* London: Hodder & Stoughton, 1951.

Clarke, Adam. *Clarke's Commentary.* New York: Methodist Book Concern, n.d.

Corlett, D. Shelby. *God in the Present Tense.* Kansas City, MO: Beacon Hill Press, 1974.

Craig, Clarence Tucker. *The Interpreter's Bible*, Vol. X. New York: Abingdon-Cokesbury Press, 1953.

Cushman, Ralph S. *I Have a Stewardship.* Nashville, TN: Abingdon Press, 1939.

Dayton, Wilbur T. "Holiness Truth in Romans." In *Further Insights into Holiness,* edited by Kenneth Geiger. Kansas City, MO: Beacon Hill Press, 1963.

Deal, William S. *Problems of the Spirit-Filled Life.* Kansas City, MO: Beacon Hill Press, 1961.

Earle, Ralph. "Consecration and Crucifixion." In *Further Insights into Holiness,* edited by Kenneth Geiger. Kansas City, MO: Beacon Hill Press, 1963.

Earle, Ralph; A. Elwood Sanner; and Charles L. Childers, eds. *Beacon Bible Commentary*, Vol. 7. Kansas City, MO: Beacon Hill Press, 1970.

Enroth, Ronald M. *Churches That Abuse.* Grand Rapids, MI: Zondervan, 1992.

Fee, Gordon. *God's Empowering Presence.* Peabody, MA: Hendrickson Publishers, 1994.

Gillquist, Peter. *Let's Quit Fighting about the Holy Spirit.* Grand Rapids, MI: Zondervan, 1974.

Greathouse, William. *Fullness of the Spirit.* Kansas City, MO: Beacon Hill Press, 1958.

Hawkinson, James R., and Robert K. Johnson, eds. *Servant Leadership, Volumes I & II.* Chicago: Covenant Publications, 1993.

Hymnal of the Church of God. Anderson, IN: Warner Press, 1971.

Hymnal of the Methodist Episcopal Church. Western Methodist Book Concern, 1878.

Hymns for the Family of God. Nashville, TN: Paragon Associates, 1976.

Kuglin, Robert. J. *Handbook of the Holy Spirit*. Camp Hill, PA: Christian Publications, 1996.

Larson, Bruce. *There's a Lot More to Health Than Not Being Sick*. Waco, TX: Word Books, 1981.

Marshall, Catherine. *The Helper*. Lincoln, VA: Chosen Books, 1978.

Missildine, W. Hugh. *Your Inner Child of the Past*. New York: Simon and Schuster, 1963.

Morgan, G. Campbell. *The Spirit of God*. London: Henry E. Walter, 1953.

Nicholson, Roy S. *Holiness and the Human Element: Insights to Holiness*. Kansas City, MO: Beacon Hill Press, 1966.

Ogilvie, Lloyd John. *Why Not? Accept Christ's Healing and Wholeness*. Old Tappan, NJ: Fleming H. Revell, 1985.

Peterson, Eugene. *A Long Obedience in the Same Direction: Discipleship in an Instant Society*. Downers Grove, IL: InterVarsity Press, 1980.

Praise and Worship: The Nazarene Hymnal. Kansas City, MO: Lillenas Publishing Company, n.d.

Ramm, Bernard L. *Rapping about the Spirit*. Waco, TX: Word Books, 1974.

Ravenhill, Leonard. *Revival Praying*. Minneapolis: Bethany Fellowship, 1962.

Special Voices Number Two, Gospel Solos and Duets. Kansas City, MO: Lillenas Publishing Company, 1958.

Sanders, J. Oswald. *The Holy Spirit and His Gifts*. Grand Rapids, MI: Zondervan, 1970.

Shoemaker, Samuel M. *With the Holy Spirit and with Fire*. Waco, TX: Word Books, 1960.

Simpson, A. B. *The Gentle Love of the Holy Spirit*. Camp Hill, PA: Christian Publications, 1983.

Smith, Oswald J. *The Enduement of Power*. London: Marshall, Morgan & Scott, n.d.

Snaith, Norman H. *The Distinctive Ideas of the Old Testament*. London: Epworth Press, 1944.

Special Voices Number 5: Sacred Solos and Duets. Kansas City, MO: Lillenas Publishing Company, 1966.

Stewart, James S. *The Wind of the Spirit*. Nashville, TN: Abingdon Press, 1968.

Stott, John R. "Studies in Ephesians." Chicago: Moody Founders Conference Series, Moody Cassette Ministry 4-12-96.

Streeter, B. H. *The Primitive Church*. New York: Macmillan, 1929.

Taylor, J. Paul. *The Music of Pentecost*. Winona Lake, IN: Light and Life Press, 1951.

Taylor, Richard Shelley. *The Disciplined Life*. Kansas City, MO: Beacon Hill Press, 1962.

Thurman, Howard. *Disciplines of the Spirit*. New York: Harper and Row, 1963.

Walvoord, John F. *The Holy Spirit*. Wheaton, IL: Van Kampen Press, 1954.

Weatherhead, Leslie D. *When the Lamp Flickers*. Nashville, TN: Abingdon Press, 1948.

Wiley, Orton. *Christian Theology, Vol II*. Kansas City, MO: Beacon Hill Press, 1952.

Wood, Laurence W. *Truly Ourselves, Truly the Spirit's*. Grand Rapids, MI: Francis Asbury Press, 1989.

———. *Pentecostal Grace*. Wilmore, KY: Francis Asbury Press, 1980.

Worship the Lord: Hymnal of the Church of God. Anderson, IN: Warner Press, 1989.

Wynkoop, Mildred Bangs. *Foundations of Wesleyan-Arminian Theology*. Kansas City, MO: Beacon Hill Press, 1967.